NEVER FORGET!

Leadership, Routinization, and Transformation in a Charismatic Organization

*From the Founder to the Successors
in the Church of God in Christ
1961-1968*

By
Robert R. Owens, Ph.D.

XULON PRESS

NEVER FORGET!
by Robert R. Owens, Ph.D.

Printed in the United States of America

Library of Congress Control Number: 2002115346
ISBN 1-591602-89-0

Xulon Press
11350 Random Hills Road
Suite 800
Fairfax, VA 22030
(703) 279-6511
XulonPress.com

To order additional copies, call 1-866-909-BOOK (2665).

Acknowledgements

First I want to acknowledge my Lord and Savior Jesus Christ whose ever-abundant grace, guidance, and support saved me, sanctified me, and filled me with His Holy Spirit.

Next, I must acknowledge the best wife in the whole world, Rev. Rosalie S. Owens, DSL. Without her life would be a dreary and lonely place. I must thank God who gave her to me for her years of encouragement and help.

My counselor throughout the writing of this work, the chairman of my dissertation committee, and a man who I see as my mentor and the best example I have ever known of a Christian educator, Dr. Vinson Synan. His advice and example continue to point the way toward credible and useful scholarship.

To Buck and Lina Bryant I offer my deepest thanks. Without your encouragement and support, this work would not be in the hands of the reader. THANK YOU!

I hesitate to make a list of the many people who have given so graciously of their time, talents, and records to contribute sources for this work because I fear I may omit someone. However, there are so many whose names must appear in this acknowledgement section I will hazard an attempt.

I thank all of you from the bottom of my heart and the depth of my soul: Superintendent Raymond Flemons, Superintendent J. Williams, Elder G. Davis, Dr. R. Johnson, Carlton, Elder C. Williams, Elder D. Duke, Dr. G. Wesley Hardy, Bishop L. Jones, Terry McCoy, Bishop C. Blake, Bishop S. P. Nesbitt, Mother C. Clemmons, all of the ladies in the Interlibrary Loan Department of Regent University and a special thanks to Alias Anonymous, all those who could agree to be interviewed but because of other considerations could not receive credit for the information they shared.

Your servant in Christ,

Robert R. Owens

Robert R. Owens, Ph.D.

Table of Contents

Dedication

In faith and with humility I dedicate this work to the glory of my Lord and Savior Jesus Christ and to that great portion of His Church, which is the Church of God in Christ (COGIC). I praise God for COGIC in my life and in the ecclesiastical history of His kingdom.

CHAPTER I

Introduction

Why is it important to study the years 1961-1968 in the history of the Church of God in Christ?

In this book these years are designated, the Dark Years, because for many people the happenings of these years have been beyond the pale of illuminating research. Research either of an historical nature or as in the case of this work their evaluation in relation to the theories, practices, and procedures of Leadership Studies.

As this study unfolds it is well to remember the popular truism, "He who fails to learn from History, is doomed to repeat it."

It is the prayer of the author that
this book will help us all to
NEVER FORGET!

COGIC has continuously ranked as America's fastest-growing denomination every year since 1982 (Maxwell, 1996, p. 22). It has consistently maintained an average gain of 600 congregations and 200,000 new members per year. Today, it is America's fifth largest denomination, more than twice the size of the Assemblies of God (the second largest Pentecostal denomination). One interesting way to judge the magnitude of this growth is to compare it to the growth of several other well-known religious bodies. Between the years 1982 and 1991 COGIC grew by 48 %, "compared to 22.3 percent for the Church of Jesus Christ of Latter Day saints, 22 percent for the Assemblies of God, 14.4 percent for the Roman Catholic Church, and 9.1 percent for the

Southern Baptist Convention" (Maxwell, 1996, p. 22).

As the fastest-growing religious body in the United States (for 17 consecutive years) the value of determining COGIC's leadership style, organizational type, and succession methods before, during and after the turmoil of the Dark Years cannot be overstated. An understanding of these events (the Dark Years), the institutions, and the processes that precipitated, endured and resolved them constitutes experiential evidence for use in developing and understanding the theories and practices of organizational leadership. The obvious desirability of organizations avoiding dislocations such as the Dark Years in the future point dramatically to the importance of this study. Until this study there has been no analysis of COGIC's Dark Years, which sought to examine the organizational leadership dimensions of these events thus, the opportunity to learn from them in this area did not exist.

One other element adds to the importance of this study. Many of the principal actors, participants and observers of the Dark Years are still living and able to provide unequaled primary sources for this research. Enough time has passed (30+ years) to allow for the heated emotions and passionate spirits of the Dark Years to have cooled, and yet the memories and observations are still sharp. To wait until these leaders have passed from the scene before attempting to chronicle and learn from them would be scholarly neglect.

In addition, five reasons provide the impetus for this study.

There is a need for a comprehensive history of COGIC leadership styles and organizational types before, during, and after the Dark Years. A review of literature reveals that there is no comprehensive history that seeks to analyze the leadership styles and organizational types that existed in COGIC before, during, and after the Dark Years. The sources are scattered and in many cases hard to access. The review of literature also reveals that there remain many unasked as well as many unanswered questions such as: What, if any, aspects of COGIC leadership style precipitated the Dark Years? What implications, for COGIC and other denominations (short- and long-term) have proceeded from the Dark Years? Can a repetition of the Dark Years be expected in COGIC's future? Can the knowledge gained from a study of COGIC's Dark Years provide insights that could help COGIC and other organizations avoid this type of trauma and disruption? This book answers these questions through the compilation and analysis of the varied sources referenced in this work.

Thus, there is a need for basic research into the Dark Years. This work compiles relevant data from diverse sources, assembled in descriptive categories, providing the basis for generalized assertions and supporting justifiable interpretations of the causes, implications and results of the Dark Years. These categories, generalizations and interpretations in turn lead to conclusions and recommendations based upon the theories and practices of organizational leadership designed to apply the lessons learned from COGIC's Dark Years.

There is a need for a general understanding of the Dark Years. This work represents the attempt to examine and learn from an experience that occurred within a major American denomination as a direct result of leadership styles and organizational types. This work also represents an effort to help organizations avoid such periods of turmoil and their resultant retrogression, schisms, and turmoil as typified by the Dark Years in the future. The avenue for this avoidance is supplied through the application of the theories and practices of organizational leadership as focused through the conclusions and recommendations developed through this case study. Finally, this work presents a model to scholars of a critical procedure useful for the assessment of past events as the platform for theoretical evaluation and practical recommendations, with the ultimate hope that these assessments, evaluations, and recommendations will subsequently serve as tools for the enrichment of future leaders and their organizations.

Concerning the Dark Years, there is a need for scholarly research for use. This work results in research for use in that it has practical applications. The questions asked in this research are designed to produce findings meant to give insight into what leadership styles and organizational types precipitated, endured and resolved the tumult and turmoil of the Dark Years. They are also designed to reveal their broader implications for the theories and practices of organizational leadership. The product of this research provides a means for making recommendations aimed at avoiding this type of disruptive interlude in the future for COGIC and other organizations.

The study of the Dark Years can make a significant contribution to Pentecostal studies. This work adds significantly to the body of Pentecostal studies by compiling and preserving the history and organizational implications of COGIC's Dark Years by gathering and organizing scattered, fragmentary, and (often) contradictory sources of information into a coherent whole. This study also presents the experience of a major American Pentecostal denomination that successfully faced schisms and turmoil after the death of its founding leader.

The study of the Dark Years and its analysis with regard to leadership theories, practices and procedures can make a contribution to organizational leadership studies. Through the scholarly compilation and evaluation of the sources referenced, both those that chronicle the events of COGIC's Dark Years and those that apply the theories and practices of organizational leadership, this work makes original contributions to the specific area of leadership studies. This is accomplished by offering insights into what leadership styles and organizational types precipitated, endured and resolved COGIC's Dark Years in an effort to show how organizations can structure themselves and their leadership in order to avoid such problems in the future.

What is the purpose of this study? The purpose of this work is to describe, interpret, and evaluate the leadership styles and organizational types present in the Church of God in Christ with respect to the period of time this work terms "the Dark Years" (1961-1968). This inquiry into the succession process following the death of Bishop C. H. Mason, the results of this process, the subsequent reorganization of the church, and the policies implemented, which directly led to the end of the Dark Years provide valuable primary research into a segment of American religious history at best overlooked, and at worst ignored by previous scholarship. This study provides explicit, valuable insights into the leadership styles, organizational types and methods of succession, which contributed to and flowed, from the Dark Years. Such insights are useful in providing guidance to organizations so that they may avoid the disruption, dislocation, and turmoil implied by the term the Dark Years.

This work uses a four-fold exploration process to actualize the above-stated purpose. First, a case study of the period and events that constitute the Dark Years is developed to gain an understanding of the leadership style, organizational type, and method of leadership succession that directly precipitated the Dark Years. Second, the case study is then used to ascertain the styles of leadership and organizational types that existed within COGIC during this period and whose evolution ultimately led to the end of the Dark Years. Third, the study is used to determine if COGIC has taken steps to avoid a recurrence of the Dark Years. Finally, this case study is used to evaluate the answers to the above objectives in reference to generalized concepts of leadership styles, organizational types, and methods of leadership succession.

What is the hypothesis this study tries to prove? The hypothesis of this work is that insights into the theories and practices of organizational leadership will be gained through a detailed study of the leadership styles and organizational types that precipitated, endured and resolved the transitional period (1961 - 1968) in the history of the Church of God in Christ, which followed the death of its founder, Bishop C. H. Mason. This is accomplished through the development of a case study of the events of these years and through the answering of specific research questions.

What are the research questions that guide this study? Research questions provide scope, order, and delimitation to any inquiry. This work uses the following questions to explore the leadership style and organizational types that precipitated, endured, and resolved COGIC's Dark Years.

1. What lessons can be learned from COGIC's Dark Years?
2. What preparation for leadership succession was taken before Bishop Mason's death?
3. What prevented an orderly transfer of power after Mason's death?
4. What type of leadership style was operating in COGIC during the Dark Years?
5. How has COGIC refined and institutionalized the succession process?

Are there any other questions that this study will attempt to answer? In an effort to gain all the knowledge possible from this case study and evaluation, in the conclusion, besides answering the above research questions this work will also answer the following six questions. Does this study support or reject the hypothesis? Does the study support or contradict previous research? Is the study conclusive or is further research needed? What are the implications of this research to the discipline? Should currently accepted research practices be redefined? Is there an accumulation of sub-answers and resolutions that give an overall answer to the research questions?

Description of Research Design

This work uses primary and secondary source documents to augment interviews of participants and observers of COGIC's Dark Years in order to reconstruct, and then analyze the leadership styles and organizational types, which precipitated, endured and eventually resolved the conflict and turmoil of this crucial period. Based upon these sources this work compares findings to the research questions. It then moves from specific data to generalizations based upon that data, and finally presents recommendations aimed at either supporting, disputing and advancing the theories and practices of organizational leadership. The primary goal is an effort to advance the understanding of how organizational leadership theories and practices are relevant to an understanding of organizational history as exemplified in a watershed experience within a major American religious denomination.

Identification of Data-gathering Method and Database of Study

The case study method has been chosen as the primary data-gathering method of this work since the desired aim is to present a detailed picture of the leadership styles and organizational types that precipitated, endured and resolved COGIC's Dark Years. The decision to pursue the case study method rests upon two factors. One, a review of pertinent literature on the subject of the Dark Years reveals that there are no dissertations, theses, or books (either scholarly or popular) dealing exclusively with this subject presently in print, leading to the conclusion by the author that the subject of the Dark Years has not received adequate coverage in scholarly literature and therefore there is a need for primary research. Two, my study in the field of research design and evaluation (as outlined below) show that the case study is the proper tool to use. Several factors have contributed to this decision.

The first factor analyzed was the definition of a case study itself. Stephen Isaac and William B. Michael in their book *Handbook in Research and Evaluation* (1981) define a case study as "in depth investigations of a given social unit resulting in a complete well organized picture of the unit" (p. 48). Several other well-known authorities in research design support this definition and its appropriateness for use in studies of this kind.

Michael Q. Patton, in his book *How To Use Qualitative Methods in Evaluation* (1987), states:

> Case studies become particularly useful where one needs to understand some particular problem or situation in great depth, and where one can identify cases rich in information – rich in the sense that a great deal can be learned from a few exemplars of the phenomenon in question. (p. 19)

David R. Krathwohl, in his book *Methods of Educational and Social Science Research* (1993), adds,

> "Case studies are bounded by a particular pro-gram, institution, time period, or set of events. Within those boundaries, whatever is the focus of attention is described in perspective to the context surrounding it" (p. 347).

In *Research Design: Qualitative & Quantitative Approaches* (1994) John W. Creswell states that appropriate uses for the case study are those:

> In which the researcher explores a single entity or phenomenon ('the case') bounded by time and activity (a program, event, process, institution, or social group) and collects detailed information by using a variety of data collection procedures during a sustained period of time. (Creswell, 1994, p. 12)

Delbert C. Miller speaks to the method used by the investigator in a case study in his book *Handbook of Research Design and Social Measurement* (1991) when he says the case study "Usually refers to relatively intense analysis of a single instance of a phenomenon being investigated" (p. 22). He also states that the "Investigator interviews individuals or studies life history documents to gain insight into behavior" (p. 22).

Another factor that contributed to the decision as to which research method to use is the consideration of how much control can be exercised over the behavior or events. This work, which is examining a set of circumstances and events that occurred in the past, will accordingly have no control over these events. According to Robert K. Yin, "the case study, which often relies on histories, has practically no control over events" (Yin, 1994, p. 23).

A third factor that contributed to the decision as to which research method should be chosen consisted of the question, "What kind of questions are the focus of the study?" This dissertation asks questions of a "How" and "Why" nature. Again according to Robert K. Yin in his book, *Case Study Research: Design and Methods* (1994), "In general, case studies are the preferred strategy when 'how' or 'why' questions are being posed, when the investigator has little control over events, and when the focus is on a contemporary phe-nomenon within some real-life context" (p. 1). The subject of questions is also addressed by John W. Creswell in his book *Research Design: Qualitative & Quantitative Approaches* (1994) where he states, "One typically finds research questions, not objectives or hypotheses, written into qualitative studies" (p. 70).

The database that provides the foundation for this work includes primary and secondary documents. The primary documents include contemporaneous Year Books of COGIC's annual Convocations, court documents, contem-poraneous newspaper accounts of the events, the record of the events as recorded in *The Whole Truth* (COGIC's official organ) and accounts written by eyewitnesses and partici-pants. Secondary documents include histories and analysis as recorded in current articles and books.

A major part of the original, primary sources for this work consists of interviews. All of the people interviewed represent contemporaneous participants and/or observers of the Dark Years or people who, because of their study or per-sonal position, have pertinent knowledge of the events. These interviews solicit views from several perspectives as a means of triangulation to provide corroborating evidence (Creswell, 1998, p. 202). These perspectives include (several each), a central (or Memphis- orientated) leader's outlook, a jurisdic-tional (or state) Bishop's outlook, a district superintendent's outlook, a pastor's outlook, and a member's outlook.

Comment on the Validity of Data

Every research method has its particular set of strengths and weaknesses.

The greatest weakness of the case study method is the possibility that biased views will have an inordinate impact on the conclusions drawn. Another weakness is that the researcher may choose the case study method itself (as well as the sources used) because of their own preconceptions. Case studies are also thought to be weak because when they look at events that involved many people they invariably represent relatively few subjects and are therefore not representative of the whole (Isaac & Michael, 1981, p. 48).

The ability to use multiple sources of information, such as interviews, documents, and artifacts constitutes one of the strengths of the case study (Yin, 1994, p. 23). Another strength of the case study resides in the use of a series of mini-case studies (multiple sources) to generalize from specific information to establish and substantiate sociological (in this case leadership) phenomenon. Robert K. Yin address this strength when he asserts that case studies are able to generalize from specific data gathered to theoretical propositions (Yin, 1994, p. 23). Yin also argues that just as multiple-experiments may be used to produce scientific propositions, multiple-case studies may be used to substantiate sociological phenomenon (Yin, 1994, p. 45).

The author does not offer the case study presented within this work (built upon the multiple-case study model) as a scientifically representative sample of a given population. It instead offers the case study as a useful tool in analyzing COGIC's Dark Years based upon the research design strengths stated above. In addition, the author does contend that case studies (built upon the multiple-case study model) may contain specific information concerning events, characteristics, and experiences useful in moving from specific to general knowledge.

Comment on the Originality and the Limitation of Data

This work provides original data gained through research of primary documents and research interviews.

Many of the primary documents reviewed within the confines of this work have never been brought together as they are here. Never before has anyone attempted to build a comprehensive overview of the Dark Years. In accordance with the author's desire to allow, the various actors in this great drama to speak for themselves many passages (some quite long) are included. This is not intended in any way to harm any of the various authors in any way. It is instead done to allow them to have a fair hearing at the Bar of History, to allow them to tell their own story, in their own words.

These interviews are ethnographic in nature in that they conform to one over-riding concept of ethnography:

Ethnographic interviewing ... begins with the assumption that the question-answer sequence is a single element in human thinking. Questions always imply answers. Statements of any kind always imply questions. This is true even when the questions and answers remain unstated. In ethnographic interviewing, *both questions and answers must be discovered from the informants.* (Spradley, 1979, p. 83-84)

While instruments were used in the interviews, each instrument was developed specifically for each individual, the order of questions was varied, and the format was always free ranging and open-ended.

This work is limited in several ways. First, it is limited since as in any research project the preconceived suppositions of the researcher may color the conclusions drawn. Moreover, as in any qualitative study, "the findings could be subject to other interpretations" (Creswell, 1994, p. 111). This work is also limited in that interviews form a substantial part of the primary research and as in all interviews, the individuals interviewed only provide the information they either remember or choose to volunteer. A further limitation of this source of primary data is the natural variations of memory and point-of-view.

Disclaimer

The author of this work **in no way** attempts to address the spiritual aspects of the Church of God in Christ. This **is not** an examination of the spirituality, biblical correctness, or appropriateness of any of the actions described. **Neither does the author of this work wish in any way to cast aspersions** upon the characters, morals, or spirituality of any person mentioned within the context of either the case study or the evaluations contained here-in. **No judgements are expressed or implied** as to the motives, objectives, or reasons associated with any of the events discussed in this work. By way of full disclosure, the author must also disclose that he is an Elder in the Church of God in Christ.

CHAPTER II

A Brief History of the Church of God in Christ

In March 1897, Charles Harrison Mason (1866-1961) made a covenant with God. At the time, Mason was an itinerant Baptist Holiness preacher. Walking down a street in Little Rock, Arkansas in 1897, Mason felt he heard God say, "If you take this name, the Church of God in Christ, there will never be a building large enough to house the people I will send you" (Clemmons, 1996, p. 11; p. 124; Cobbins, 1969, p. 431; Patterson, Ross and Atkins, 1969, p. 63; the Official Manual of the Church of God in Christ, 1973, p. XXVI). Bishop Mason accepted this as a direction from God and consequently proposed the name for the new Holiness church he and C. P. Jones were founding at that time. Since then the Church of God in Christ (COGIC) has experienced phenomenal growth.

In an effort to advance the understanding of organizational leadership theory and practice and to broaden its impact upon church life, this work focuses on the events that surrounded the disputed leadership succession which followed the death of Bishop C. H. Mason in 1961. For about a decade (1961-1968) this major American denomination struggled through personality conflicts, court battles, and self-examination as it sought to define itself in the post-Mason era.

How C. H. Mason Laid the Cornerstone of the Church of God in Christ

The first sermon Bishop C. H. Mason preached in 1893 in Preston, Arkansas dealt with holiness. This sermon convicted people of their sins and converted many to the Gospel of Jesus Christ. Here, at the beginning of his ministry, Bishop Mason also taught that sin was the cause of all sickness and disease (Clemmons, 1996, p. 5; Mason, 1987, p. 23-24; Paterson et al., 1969, p. 15-16).

The ministry of another member of the National Baptist Convention, Charles Price Jones (1865-1947) who was the pastor of Mt. Helm Baptist Church in Jackson, Mississippi, brought C. H. Mason deeper into holiness teachings. Jones undertook "deeper spiritual labors" (Clemmons, 1996, p.13; Pleas, 1991, p. 1) in an effort to propagate the belief in Christian perfection among the members of the National Baptist Convention. Jones and Mason taught the Wesleyan doctrine of "Complete or Total" sanctification (Synan, 1997, p. 169) as a second work of grace. They based these teachings on Mathew 5:48, "Therefore you shall be perfect, just as your Father in heaven is perfect" (Clemmons, 1996, p. 13). These holiness teachings became the cause for debate and divisiveness within the bounds of the Calvinistic National Baptist Convention.

After Jones convened his first Holiness Convention at Mt. Helm Baptist Church at Jackson, Mississippi on June 6, 1897, Mason and Jones became co-laborers and worked tirelessly to spread holiness doctrines (Clemmons, 1996, p.8-9). They soon found themselves sought after as speakers throughout the mid-south. The influence and reputations of the two young evangelists grew until 1899 when the National Baptist Convention expelled them because of their teachings (Cobbins, 1969, p. 29). Having previously founded the Church of God in Christ (1897), they proceeded to establish this as a separate denomination with C. P. Jones as the General Overseer and Mason as the Overseer of Tennessee (Cobbins, 1969, p. 28; Pleas, 1991, p. 6). (An interesting sidebar to this generally accepted and oft-cited statement is the fact that there is no record of COGIC being legally incorporated prior to 1922 in Tennessee.)

In 1907, C. H. Mason visited the Azusa Street Revival and received the baptism with the Holy Spirit accompanied by the initial evidence of speaking in tongues (Cobbins, 1969, p. 431; Pleas, 1991, p. 6-7; COGIC Manual, 1973, p. XXVI-XXVI). This was a life-changing event in Bishop Mason's life and ministry. Mason had accepted the theological position espoused by Elder William J. Seymour (1872-1922), leader of the Azusa Street Mission. This theology, derived from the teachings of Charles F. Parham (1873-1929), taught that speaking in tongues constituted the "only" initial evidence of the baptism with the Holy Ghost (Burgess et al., 1988, p. 660; Mason, 1987, p. 26-30; Synan, 1997, p. 91).

Leaving Azusa Street, instead of going directly home to Memphis, Tennessee, Mason traveled to the Tidewater area of Virginia (Clemmons, 1996, p. 64; Synan, 1997, p. 125; Morring, 1996, p. 17). According to oral traditions, this was an area where he had long been an active apostle (J. Williams, personal communication, July 15, 1999). He stopped first at a small holiness church he had previously brought into COGIC in the Chuckatuck area of Suffolk County, Friendship Cathedral, where he preached the baptism in the Holy Ghost.

A revival broke out in response to his preaching. Many people gave their lives to the Lord and received the Pentecostal baptism, and there was great excitement. News spread from tobacco fields to peanut fields in the rural areas of southeast Virginia. People came from as far away as Norfolk and the church in Chuckatuck was greatly increased. At this time, Elder Mason told the people they should refrain from the activities associated with the 300th anniversary of Jamestown. He also told them that if they would instead fast and pray the Lord would greatly bless the saints and the City of Norfolk (J. Williams, personal communication, July 15, 1999).

After leaving Chuckatuck, Elder Mason and several other leaders from that area traveled to Norfolk to spread the new Pentecostal message. The first place they went was the old Grant Street Church where he usually attended when visiting the Tidewater area. After he preached a sermon on the baptism in the Holy Ghost and shared about his experiences at Azusa Street, the leaders asked him and his companions to leave that church (Williams, 1991, p. 23).

Bishop Mason was about to continue on to Memphis when he felt the Holy Ghost tell him to stay and preach the message of Pentecost. Having no church open to him, he started a street ministry in downtown Norfolk in April 1907. Bishop Mason preached on the street outside the Ferry Terminal on Commercial Place. This built on earlier work done by Lucy Farrow, one of the pioneer evangelists to leave Azusa Street for Africa. This mighty woman of God had preached the Pentecostal message in Portsmouth and Norfolk in 1906 (Noble, 1985, p. 7).

Many people scorned and ridiculed Bishop Mason when he started preaching on the street. The police threatened him with arrest, but they never did arrest him. In addition, although this was in the nadir of Jim Crow Laws, numerous Caucasians attended the meetings and responded to Mason's call for salvation, sanctification, and baptism with the Holy Ghost. Estimates of the number saved during this revival vary between 6,000 (Clemmons, 1996, p. 64), several thousand (Synan, 1997, p. 125), and 600 (J. Williams, personal communication, July 15, 1999; Young, 1991, p. 14) during this 1907 revival. The variance in these figures aptly represents the numerous contradictions found in many of the early reports and stories based upon different streams of oral traditions.

After the street preaching had gathered in this large number of converts, both African-American and Caucasian, Bishop Mason started holding meetings in private homes. As more and more people continued to respond to the Pentecostal message they soon needed larger facilities. Staying in Norfolk, he first rented a storefront on Monticello Avenue, then a larger one on St. Paul Street and then a still larger one on Cumberland Street. Before Elder Mason left for Memphis, he organized the saints who had been saved in the revival into a church with himself as the pastor. Within a short time they purchased a lot on Goff Street and built the first church, which was to become the C. H. Mason Memorial Church of God in Christ. This church is now known as the "Mother" church because it has been the seedbed for so many preachers, pastors, bishops and churches (Williams, 1991, p. 23; J. Williams, personal communication, July 15, 1999).

Bishop Mason finally felt that the Holy Ghost would allow him to continue his journey home to Memphis. He arrived in Memphis in late July, just in time to visit his own church and to prepare to make his way to the Holy Convocation of the Church of God in Christ for 1907. Mason was surprised to find that he was not the first person to preach the message of Azusa Street to his own church in Memphis. He was proceeded by Glen Cook (1867-1948), a veteran of the great revival who had served as Elder Seymour's business manager. Brother Cook was in the middle of an across-the-country evangelistic tour spreading the word of the Pentecostal revival (Clemmons, 1996, p. 64; Synan, 1986, p. 47).

It was at the 1907 Convocation that Bishop Mason presented his case for the Baptism with the Holy Ghost, as taught at Azusa Street by Elder W. J. Seymour. General Overseer of the Church of God in Christ, C. P. Jones opposed his efforts at the convocation in August of 1907 in Jackson, Mississippi. The General Overseer "regarded the new Holy Ghost experience of speaking in tongues as a delusion" (Hall, 1995, p. 12). C. P. Jones thought that COGIC should remain a Holiness church and reject the new Pentecostal teachings, thus forming a united front with other Holiness denominations such as the Church of God (Anderson, IN), The Salvation Army, The Christian and Missionary Alliance, and the Nazarene Church (Clemmons, 1996, p. 65; Cobbins, 1966, p. 432-433).

Mason attempted to lead the entire Church of God in Christ into the new Pentecostal mold. But Jones, who controlled the convocation, demanded that Mason soften his position to say that speaking in tongues was merely "one" of the initial evidences of the baptism with the Holy Ghost (Clemmons, 1996, p. 65). Mason refused to do this so the General Overseer and the Convocation "withdrew from C. H. Mason and all who promulgated the doctrine of speaking with tongues the right hand of fellowship" (Cobbins, 1969, p. 432; see also: Hall, 1995, p. 12; Synan, 1997, p. 126).

When Mason left the Convocation approximately half of the delegates went with him. Mason sent out a letter to all the members of the Church telling them of his experience and asking that they meet with him in Memphis in September of 1907 (Cobbins, 1969, p. 432; Clemmons, 1996, p. 65). This meeting was convened as the "Pentecostal Assembly of the Church of God in Christ" (Clemmons, 1996, p. 66). At this meeting, the delegates elected Mason as the Chief Apostle of the church (COGIC Manual, 1973, p. XXIX). This Assembly also amended the Articles of Religion of the church by adding a "Pentecostal paragraph" (Synan, 1997, p. 126). COGIC at the same time retained a belief in sanctification. This Holiness-Pentecostal mix was expressed in a statement added to the official manual of the church, "We therefore, believe that before a believer can be filled with the Holy Ghost, he must first be sanctified," (COGIC Manual, 1973, p. 58).

With these actions, the split between the Holiness and the Pentecostal wings of the Church of God in Christ became permanent. A court battle raged for two years to decide which faction had the exclusive right to use the name and charter of the church (Clemmons, 1996, p. 66; Cobbins, 1969, p. 433). The court of Shelby County, Tennessee decided in favor of the Pentecostal Assembly on May 15, 1909. According to an article entitled "Opinion" which appeared in *The Whole Truth* (April 1968), this ruling was based upon the fact that the Church of God in Christ was not at that time legally incorporated:

It is insisted on behalf of the complainants that the church to which the defendants and complainants belong is a member of an association of churches under control of a superior council ... It has no authority whatever over the individual churches. Its action can only be in any case advisory.

Indeed we do not think that any council has ever been organized. It appears that in January 1906, there was a meeting of ministers of various colored churches professing sanctification; and there was again a meeting in August 1906. At this meeting there was present the pastor of the church of South Wellington Street Memphis, [Mason] which is the subject of the present controversy and also a member - one Murphy. The evidence, however, fails to show that either of these persons was commissioned to place the church under the authority of the alleged superior council, nor does it appear that there was such authority conferred upon other person present.

It appears that the two meetings in Jackson, Mississippi, above referred to were what is called "holiness" meetings composed largely of ministers of that persuasion. It is true that while these men were present, they undertook to effect some kind of organization and appointed three men whom they called overseers, C. P. Jones' supposed jurisdiction was the State of Mississippi, Mason's, the State of Tennessee, Jeter's the State of Arkansas. Their powers according to Jones, consisted principally in watching over the churches and seeing that no improper ministers officiated. It required two of them to authorize a minister to act as such, and it seems they assumed the authority to dispose of ministers also.

We cannot find in the record any sufficient evidence that this authority was conferred upon these men by the churches. We are likewise unable to find in the record any sufficient evidence that the alleged superior council had conferred upon it any authority by the churches; certainly not by the congregation whose church is in controversy in the present case.

We think the overwhelming weight of evidence shows that the defendants' [Mason's] church belongs to the congregational order, and that it is not subject to oversight by any superior ecclesiastical organization. (p. 6)

Because COGIC was not incorporated at the time of this dispute, Mason was able to maintain control of the name Church of God in Christ. The Holiness wing of the church now reorganized as Church of Christ (Holiness) USA (Cobbins, 1969, p. 30, 435; Clemmons, 1996, p. 66).

Mason insisted on retaining the worship and prayer traditions of slave religion, which included the prayer circle, lively worship (such as shouting, jumping), and the "Holy Dance" (For further information on Slave Religion see *The Cultural Renewal of Slave Religion,* the dissertation of D. D. Daniels, III, Ph.D., Union Theological Seminary, 1992.) At the same time, he led the church in developing a new Pentecostal spirituality. Mason's leadership moved COGIC from the inward focus on personal perfection of the Holiness Movement to an outward focus that saw the social suffering of the oppressed as something that the Christian community should address and ameliorate. COGIC grew rapidly after the split and was soon the largest African-American Pentecostal denomination in the world (Clemmons, 1996, p. 34-35; Synan, 1997, p. 126).

Although "the Church of God in Christ saw a link between religious practice and racial identity" (Clemmons, 1996, p. 70), Elder Mason, deeply affected by his experience of the profoundly inter-racial revival at Azusa Street (Owens, 1998, p. 105), welcomed the many white ministers who were routinely thrown out of their churches and denominations once they had received the baptism with the Holy Spirit. As a legally recognized church the clergy who held their credentials from COGIC were able to obtain railway passes, perform marriages and other official functions (Synan, 1997, p. 171). Thus Mason, "Through his practice of ordaining ministers of all races ... acted as a conduit for the fire of the Azusa Street Revival to all parts of the United States" (Owens, 1998, p. 85).

Mason is considered "a race-transcending prophet – someone who never forgot the significance of race but refused to be confined to a race" (Clemmons, 1996, p. 71). Although highly unusual for the times this aspect of the reorganized COGIC manifested itself in the fact that between 1907 and 1914 Bishop Mason ordained 350 white ministers (Clemmons, 1996, p. 70). As a result of this practice, between 1907 and 1914 there came to be as many white ministers in COGIC as there were African-American. "At times, Mason referred to the white group of ministers in the Church of God in Christ as the 'White work of the Church' " (Synan, 1997, p. 171). However "By 1913 it had become increasingly clear that as Pentecostals moved toward denominationalism, they would follow the segregating practices of American culture" (Burgess, McGee & Alexander, 1988, p. 587).

In 1913 elders E. N. Bell (1866-1923) and H. A. Goss (1883-1864) sent invitations stating that a general council of "all pentecostal saints and Churches of God in Christ" (Bugess, McGee & Alexander, 1988, p. 587) would convene in April 1914 in Hot Springs, Arkansas. "This invitation went only to the white saints. E. N. Bell's periodical, *Word and Witness*, was not distributed in the black religious community" (Burgess et al., 1988, p. 587). Following this call and the meetings which flowed from it the majority of COGIC's white ministers left in 1914 to found the Assemblies of God. Historian Robert M. Anderson states that "no hostility, racial or other seems to have been involved" (Anderson, 1992, p. 189) in this split. The only evidence Anderson presents of this attitude, "Bishop Mason addressed that organizing meeting and gave his blessing to the new denomination," (Anderson, 1992, p. 189) appears to express Mason's attitude toward the seceding white clergy. However, it does not reveal the attitude of those who left, except collaterally in that they invited him to speak. Another indication of Bishop Mason's view of race relations within the church can be seen in one of his favorite sayings, "The church is like the eye: it has a little black in it and a little white in it, and without both it can't see" (Maxwell, 1996, p. 5).

Bishop Ithiel Clemmons (1992) addresses the issue of why the whites left by stating, "According to white scholars, they left because the larger society, especially in the South, refused to modify its worship patterns to accommodate whites. Moreover, whites became restive when they could not assume the prevailing leadership role" (p. 70-71). Clemmons (1992) also sates that "White American pentecostalism and neo-pentecostalism, at least since 1914, employed segregationist politics and racist attitudes similar to those of greater North American society" (p. 36-37).

Addressing the impact of this exodus of whites from COGIC Vinson Synan says, "The formation of the Assemblies of God was of crucial importance to the future development of the Pentecostal movement, effectively marking the end of a notable experiment in interracial development" (Synan, 1997, p. 155). Bugess, McGee, and Alexander (1988) sum up the desertion of the whites by paraphrasing Frank Bartleman's famous quote, "The color line that had been washed away in the blood of Jesus at the Azusa Street revival reappeared" (p. 587).

When Bishop C. H. Mason died on November 17, 1961 he had led the denomination longer (1897-1961) than any other religious organizational leader in American history (Clemmons, 1992, p. 126). His long service at the helm left an indelible mark as the denomination that he loved and labored over lurched into the future through a period of time that this dissertation terms "The Dark Years." (This term refers to the historical veil and pall of understanding drawn by avoidance and the passage of time upon these events).

CHAPTER III

The Situation
at the Time of
Bishop Mason's Death

"For David, after he had served his own generation by the will of God, fell on sleep, and was laid unto his fathers, and saw corruption" (Acts 13:36). With this verse Bishop O. T. Jones, Sr. eulogized Bishop C. H. Mason, setting the tone for Bishop Mason's memorial and perhaps, since there was no Solomon waiting in the wings, prophetically pointing the way toward the organizational Rehobaoms and Jeroboams of the future.

From its inception at the Pentecostal Assembly of the Church of God in Christ in September 1907 until his death on November 17, 1961 for more than 54 years, Bishop C. H. Mason led the Church of God in Christ as its Chief Apostle, Senior Bishop and General Overseer. Mason led COGIC longer than any other denominational founder in modern history and this long tenure left the imprint of his beliefs and personality indelibly stamped on the life and thought of the Church (Clemmons, 1996, p. 126).

What type of leader was Bishop C. H. Mason? According to the unanimous testimony of all those who knew him, he was a charismatic leader. The social scientist Max Weber first described this type of leader. According to Weber, the charismatic leader is one whose authority rests on supposedly supernatural, or superhuman or at least specifically exceptional powers or qualities (Pugh, Hickson, 1993, p. 3-4). Throughout his life, Bishop Mason was a much beloved leader affectionately known as "Dad" to his followers (Nesbitt, 1965, p. 3; J. Williams, personal conversation, July, 15, 1999).

What type of organization did this type of leadership create? Charismatic leadership, or as Morgan (1997) calls it, "domination" (p. 303) occurs when a leader's rule exists solely by virtue of his personal qualities. The legitimacy of such an organization rests upon the faith, which the ruled put in the leader. The organization that flows from such a situation is charismatic, by nature usually unstructured or loose (Morgan, 1997, p. 305). That it was recognized by COGIC's leaders and members as a charismatic organization built around a charismatic leader is evident from such statements as:

> The reorganized Church of God in Christ, unlike many denominations, was created not so much by existing congregations coming together from the grass roots to form a national denomination, as by the efforts of one charismatic and visionary leader. (Clemmons, 1996, p. 73)

But what style of leadership did Bishop Mason use? Bishop Mason exercised an unbounded, autocratic authority that COGIC accepted, due to his charismatic presence, as being a unique gift of God to the denomination. Using the political metaphor, as developed by Gareth Morgan in his seminal work, *Images of Organization* (1997), the autocratic leader exhibits an, "absolute government where power is held by an individual or small group and supported by control of critical resources, property or ownership rights, tradition, charisma, and other claims to personal privilege" (p. 157).

This unquestioned acceptance, based upon an attitude, which bordered on veneration that surrounded Bishop

Mason, explains how he was able to maintain his absolute control of his ever-growing denomination. The perception of Bishop Mason's unique charisma, his leadership style and the absolute nature of it, finds ample expression in the writings of many COGIC authors, several of whom are quoted here as examples. In *History and the Formative Years of the Church of God in Christ*, the editors quote Elder C. G. Brown's description of Mason as:

> God's choice for the leadership of his people, kind but firm, compassionate Christ-like, touched with a feeling of our infirmities. His demeanor was that of one who desired not the praise of men but rather to be seen in reality as he was, a spirit-filled vessel with sufficient faith to be used to the glory of God with all power and authority; one who believed God always, and rested on the assurance that God would not fail him in any wise. (Patterson, et al., 1969, p. 55)

Another source described the unique nature of Bishop Mason's leadership saying, "By divine inspiration and revelation the late Bishop C. H. Mason, by precept and example, gave leadership to the Church of God in Christ for more than fifty-four years" (Nesbitt, 1965, p. 2). This same source tells how Bishop Mason used his interpretation of the Bible as the only source of written rule and in so doing revealed the absolute nature of his leadership:

> The Holy Bible was the rule book which he used to guide the Church, and even when *he granted permission* [emphasis added] for the Official Manual of the Church of God in Christ to be published, it was made clear in the said Manual that "We hold the holy scriptures as contained in the Old and New

Testaments as our sole rule of faith and practice."
(Nesbitt, 1965, p. 2)

Continuing in his description of Mason's leadership style,
Elder Samuel P. Nesbitt, the "Executive Secretary and Special
Advisor to Senior Bishop O. T. Jones" (Nesbitt, 1965, p. 16)
in his *The COGIC VOICE* (1965) addresses Mason's rela-
tionship to the people he appointed as subordinates and indirectly his use of the Bible to legitimize his actions:

> The Lord led Bishop Mason to choose certain
> men and women for special positions and functions
> in the Church. He respected their ideas, abilities and
> rights, but at no time did he allow anyone to take the
> authority which God had given him. Whenever it
> appeared that various actions or proposed programs
> for the Church were not pursuant to the Holy
> Scriptures, he was alert to check them in the spirit of
> Love. (p. 2)

Mary Mason, in her recompilation of *The History and
Life Work of Bishop C. H.Mason* (1987), also quoted Elder
C. G. Brown and revealed the depth of reverence accorded
Bishop Mason:

> I saw too that his judgement of men is not merely
> based upon a knowledge of them or the spirit of man
> which is in him but it rests upon the proper distribu-
> tion of the knowledge as is given him of God
> through the Holy Ghost. That is *one of the many*
> [emphasis added] reasons why his judgement is
> *unquestionable* [emphasis added]. (p. 85)

Under the sub-heading, Supernatural Qualities, Mary
Mason quotes Elder Brown as saying:

It is not robbery to say that Elder Mason is an apostle *with divine qualities* [emphasis added] comparing favorably with those of the apostle of the early church both in demonstration of the Spirit and of power. Assuredly, he is anointed *over and above his fellows* [emphasis added]. The manifestations of these powers is clear, plain and simple in unfolding the mystery of godliness; yet it is so wonderful, so uplifting and enlightening that everywhere it is acknowledged to be beyond the scope of the natural mind. *It is supernatural – God using his vessel to convince the world of sin, of righteousness and of judgment* [emphasis added].

As to healing, the working of miracles and casting out devils the cases are too numerous to mention. The beneficiaries of these wonderful gifts, working through him could better tell, and are telling, of the effects in their own words all over the country. (p. 56-57)

The final sentence (below) which ends the foregoing quote shows how far some people were willing to go in identifying Bishop Mason, his spirituality (and thereby his authority) with Christ and thus with a special charisma:

That same Christ-mind which commanded the lame to walk, called Lazarus from the tomb and ordered life back into the dead body of the only son of the widow of Nain, *is being demonstrated in much the same manner through our General Overseer and Chief Apostle, Elder C. H. Mason* [emphasis added]. (p. 57)

This veneration, which bordered upon worship, is shown as continuing after the death of Bishop Mason in an article which appeared in the *Tri-State Defender* (December 12, 1964):

The National Evangelist Department of the Church of God in Christ has purchased the original home of Bishop Charles H. Mason at 1121 Mississippi Blvd. in an effort to preserve the effects of the late founder of the church ... Enshrined, but without charge [*sic*], will be the late church leader's private room. The only things to be added to the room will be *a golden alter and an "Eternal Light,"* (emphasis added) as a symbol of the Bishop's message ... The first *pilgrimage* (emphasis added) to the site where the founder of the Church of God in Christ lived, prayed and was said to have received "visions from God" was made last Friday afternoon at 4:30 p. m. Thousands of delegates attending the 57th annual convocation are expected to visit the *enshrined* (emphasis added) home. ("Church Pays," 1964)

Organizations that grow and operate under charismatic leadership display an administrative apparatus that is very loose, unstructured, and therefore unstable. The charismatic leader usually begins by ruling as an autocrat and ends by working through the activities of a few disciples or intermediaries (Morgan, 1997, p. 305). COGIC replicates this pattern in the evolution of Bishop Mason's last years.

For the declining years of Bishop Mason and the period of transition that follows, there exist several streams of documentation. These streams of documentation represent the various sides in the turmoil of the Dark Years, a somewhat independent (though denominationally sanctioned) stream which attempts to remain objective, and one that provides the official quality of public documents. The first stream is representative of the O. T. Jones, Sr. faction as presented by Samuel P. Nesbitt. The second is representative of the Executive Council and is articulated (chiefly) by Bishop J. O. Patterson. The third stream, which attempts to present a balanced, objective view, resides in the work of the denominational Historical Recording Secretary, Evangelist Lucille J. Cornelius, and other contemporaneous observers. A fourth and final stream of documentation exists in the court records of the Chancery Court of Shelby County, Tennessee and in the pages of contemporaneous newspapers. This stream constitutes the public reporting of the events, and the legal compilation of the various vehicles of litigation, which chronicled the disputes and eventually pointed the way to their resolution. In the following summary of these years, this work references all of these various streams in its search for insight into the theories and practices of organizational leadership with regard to leadership styles and organizational types as exemplified in this case study.

Before and after Bishop Mason died, it had been assumed that another person would be chosen to succeed him. That this discussion of what the COGIC organization would look like after Mason's passing and who would be the new Senior Bishop did take place is reflected in an article published in the Memphis World (November 25, 1961):

> Since the bishop's serious illness and his ultimate death there has been much discussion over the future of the church. Many are wondering if the church will continue as a giant organization and many are wondering who will be named to take over leadership of the worldwide body. There are several prominent bishops in the denomination and several of them are based in Memphis. (4)

But that there was confusion as to how this would be accomplished or how it might come about is also reflected in the pages of the Memphis World (December 9, 1961):

Will the operation and administration of the world-wide Church of God in Christ continue as directed by Bishop Charles H. Mason ... Will the Executive Commission of Bishops continue to work as a body carrying on the work of the church or is there one in this group who will rise to the top and become supreme leader? ... The late Bishop Mason was the founder and Senior Bishop of the many winged Church of God in Christ ... He was the supreme leader, he was the man who called the signals, the man who made the big decisions and commitments, the man who kept the church on a steady course. ... There are many who believe that the denomination may not continue to exist as a strong force if it does not have one man at the top with dictatorial power. ... The of Church of God in Christ is now under the Executive Commission ...Many of the Church of God in Christ followers believe the present executive commission of bishops will make an honest effort to work together in interest of the church for at least three years. Others believe that there will be no effort made to change the present structure until after the chairman and co-chairman pass off the scene. And there are a few who predict that one of the bishops in the church will rise to complete power as known by Bishop Mason in less than three years. (p. 1 & 4)

In the interest of fairness to all sides in the "power struggle" (DuBois, 1966, p. 8; Synan, 1986, p. 55; Thomas, 1966, p.1) the author of this work wishes to give each stream the opportunity to present itself to the reader in its own (unedited) words through the following lengthy excerpts (the original formatting, including spacing, italics and bold print is followed where ever possible).

Bishop J. O. Patterson in the forward to his booklet *Official* (1967) states:

> Since the death of the sainted founder and father of our great church, the revered Bishop C. H. Mason, there has been much widespread confusion over the question of leadership. Many letters, brochures, and newspaper articles have been circulated, much of which has been false and inadequate information. There are those who are seeking to conquer our church by division, others with selfish motives and desires are capitalizing on our unrest, and although some of them know differently, they are willing to sacrifice every Christian principle for their own personal gain. This widespread false information has put many questions in the minds of our membership, such as:
>
> 1. Is the Executive Board the duly elected authority of the Church?
> 2. Was "Bishop" O. T. Jones elected to succeed Bishop Mason?
> 3. Is "Bishop" Jones being mistreated as the "Senior Bishop of the Church?"
> 4. Is the Executive Board one and the same as the Board of Bishops mentioned in the Constitution?
> 5. Were "Bishop" Jones and "Bishop" Ranger tried and deposed of their offices without due notice and a fair trial?
> 6. Was "Bishop" Jones denied the privilege of speaking in the 1966 National Convocation?
> 7. If "Bishop" Jones was elected only as the honorary or ceremonial head of the Church, did the Executive Board respect him in that capacity?

As General Secretary and keeper of the Church's records, without being prejudiced in the matter, I have been impressed of the Lord to put the record in print and let you judge for yourself. The Bible says, "Ye shall know the truth and the truth shall make you free."

Most of the ministers and laymen of the Church of God in Christ love the Church dearly and are grieved with the unrest that is being fertilized by those who seem to not be concerned about the general welfare of the Church but concerned with their preeminence. "For as much as many have taken in hand to set forth in order a declaration of those things which are most surely believed among us, even as they delivered them unto us, which from the beginning were eyewitnesses, and ministers of the word, it seemed good to me also, having had perfect understanding of all things from the beginning, to write to thee in order, most excellent Theophilus that thou mightest [sic] know the certainty of those things" Luke 1:1. (Patterson, 1967, Foreword)

And Samuel P. Nesbitt, who was the author of *THE COGIC VOICE* (1965) (S. Nesbitt, personal communication, December, 10, 1999), explicitly states the purpose for his writing in a section entitled "Our Purpose:"

To help the members of the Church Of God In Christ, at all levels, and all those persons who seek to know our Church, to gain the proper perspective of and a deeper insight into the true nature of the Church Of God In Christ, by publishing this factual, written record of these vital experiences and events which have brought us, under God, to the place in history where we now stand.

Without prejudice or desire for any personal gain or benefit, we seek only to present the **TRUTH**. It is our belief that once we have the **TRUTH** we will follow it. If we follow the **TRUTH**, we shall be made free from misunderstanding, resentment, offenses, falsehood, deception and sin. *"Ye shall know the truth, and the truth shall make you free."* (John. 8:32)

In the spirit of humility we have undertaken this task. By prayer, fasting, study, conference and divine counsel we have been directed to proceed to "make the vision clear" in the manner as is hereinafter set forth.

In order that our purpose might be realized, we ask that you read the material prayerfully. God will reveal the **TRUTH** to you. When the **TRUTH** is revealed, let God inspire you to follow it.

Yours for the **TRUTH** - no matter where it leads, **The COGIC VOICE.** (p. 2)

According to Bishop J. O. Patterson in his booklet Official (1967):

On June 5, 1951, the late Bishop C. H. Mason selected three men, namely Bishop A. B. McEwen, Bishop J. S. Bailey, and Bishop O. M. Kelly as his assistants and gave them power-of-attorney [no evidence of this power-of-attorney has been uncovered by the author]. They were referred to as the Special Committee. These men served as Bishop Mason's assistants until May 19, 1952 at which time the fourth person, Bishop J. O. Patterson was added. These four men served as Bishop Mason's assistants and were referred to as the Special Commission, later the Executive Commission. (p. 1)

According to Nesbitt from the beginning of 1955, Bishop Mason started to curtail his schedule. He no longer traveled as much as he had done previously. He also began to delegate more power to his direct subordinates in the areas of decisions and appointments. He chose seven men to act as what he called, "My Special Committee, or Commission" (Nesbitt, 1965, p. 3; Cornelius, 1975, p. 79). At first, Mason informally passed his authority to this Commission but then near the end of that same year Bishop Mason had the following power-of-attorney prepared:

To the members of the Church of God in Christ, Greetings:

The undersigned, your Senior Bishop and General Overseer, deems it advisable and in the interest of the prompt, efficient and benevolent continuance of all the duties of the undersigned, to appoint and authorize the following brethren, namely, Bishop O. T. Jones of Philadelphia, PA., Bishop Samuel Crouch of Los Angeles, Calif., and Bishop U. E. Miller of Detroit, Mich., to serve with the present Committee known as my Special Committee or Commission, namely Bishop A. B. McEwen, Bishop J. S. Bailey, Bishop O. M. Kelly and Bishop J. O. Patterson.

Their duties are to act collectively or individually with the present committee, in the name, stead and place of the undersigned, and in all matters which otherwise would require the attention and action of the undersigned.

The above mentioned parties hereby are invested with the power and authority from the undersigned to represent and act for the undersigned in all matters and things relating to the work of the Church of God in Christ which the undersigned himself, by reason of the pressure of his many duties, cannot attend to and discharge for the best interests of the officers and members of the Church of God in Christ.

The undersigned shall continue in the active discharge of the duties of his office and the privilege of his calling, and it is not intended by the authority hereby given to the above mentioned parties to assign or delegate to the said parties any duties or services which the undersigned desires to perform in the exercise of his office as Senior Bishop and General Overseer of the Church of God in Christ.

Bishop J. S. Bailey will serve as Co-Chairman for this committee. (Nesbitt, 1965, p. 2-3)

This document was executed in Memphis, Tennessee. Bishop Mason signed this power-of-attorney and Bishop U. E. Miller witnessed it on October 12, 1955. Bishop Patterson in his booklet *Official* (1967) refers to this same occurrence by saying:

On October 12, 1955 three others were added, namely Bishop U. E. Miller, Bishop S. M. Crouch, and Bishop O. T. Jones. They continued to serve as the Executive Commission making all appointments and performing all other acts which otherwise had been done by the late Senior Bishop C. H. Mason. (p. 1)

According to Samuel Nesbitt (1965), due to this arrangement from 1955 "trouble was started in many sections of the Church" (p. 3). As Bishop Mason became more and more incapacitated by age, and he was not able to continue the almost constant rounds of visits and speaking engagements that had always been a vital part of his highly personal, charismatic/autocratic style of leadership he entrusted an ever-growing field of authority to his commissioners. Therefore, his lieutenants became increasingly emboldened. By the close of the decade of the fifties these commissioners were traveling around the country effectively running the Church with little or no guidance. One situation that worked to cause confusion was that some of the commissioners felt that the commission had been empowered both collectively and individually. Consequently, some of the commissioners began acting individually in the area of appointments and other important decisions (Nesbitt, 1965, p. 3).

It was during this period (1955-1961) that COGIC began to experience trouble in many areas of its ecclesiastical life. The Commission (acting collectively and individually) began to enter into agreements, which created obligations and in some instances debts, which accrued to the Church as a whole. In some cases the rights and privileges of state bishops, pastors, and local churches were disregarded and infringed upon. But when the aggrieved parties appealed to the office of the Senior Bishop the matters were often referred to the Commission who rendered decisions that were perceived by some as being contrary to the accepted rules of the Church. Another problem that beset the Commission at this time was that there was a general lack of agreement among the commissioners with regard to whether or not such actions should (or could) be taken by individuals as opposed to corporate action by the Commission as a whole (Nesbitt, 1965, p. 3).

CHAPTER IV

The Circumstances Surrounding the Initial Succession and Era of Bishop O. T. Jones, Sr. as COGIC's Senior Bishop

Moses My servant is dead. Now therefore, arise, go over this Jordan, you and all this people, to the land which I am giving them ... No man shall be able to stand before you all the days of your life; as I was with Moses, so will I be with you. I will not leave you nor forsake you. Be strong and of good courage for to this people you shall divide as an inheritance the land which I swore to their fathers to give them. (Joshua 1:2,5,6)

As outlined above, by the mid-1950s Bishop Mason realized he was no longer able to be as active as he had once been. Consequently, he set up the Commission. He went so far as to sign a power-of-attorney (1955) giving the Commission the authority to take certain actions that had previously been the sole province of the Senior Bishop. Nevertheless, in all of this, he did not establish any kind of regular method of succession. He made no appointment of a First Assistant. He adopted no one as his auxiliary Senior

Bishop. So there was no Heir Apparent to step into his position and continue a seamless administration into the future. This is a clear example of Mason's charismatic authority and autocratic leadership style. He sought to use the talents and energy of his inner circle but he kept the lines of power unquestionably in his own hands.

Because of this continued one-man rule, at the death of the founder, COGIC entered a period of organizational drift. When Bishop Mason died, all personal authority, that had existed during his life, died with him. His Special Committee or Commission as an agency of authority in the Church also died with him (Nesbitt, 1965, p. 3).

COGIC's replacement of one leader by another evokes the political metaphor as described by Morgan in his book *Images of Organization* (1997) when he states:

By recognizing that organization is intrinsically political, in the sense that ways must be found to create order and direction among people with potentially diverse and conflicting interests, much can be learned about the problems and legitimacy of management as a process of government and about the relation between organization and society. (p. 153-214)

In most churches the idea of political organizations and political maneuvering (as revealed through the lens of the political metaphor) is dismissed as being too worldly for the Body of Christ (Paul's metaphor for the organization of the Church, I Corinthians 12:12-27). This is unfortunate because it does not reflect the reality of transitional organizational leadership. This dismissal of the political metaphor also prevents people from recognizing that politics and politicking may be an essential part of deciding who will be the next leader and it is therefore not necessarily an optional or dysfunctional set of actions. And since people dismiss politics as unbecoming of the Body of Christ those who decide to use political means to accomplish their purposes must work under the cover of other more acceptable motives.

According to leadership experts Sydney Finkelstein and Donald C. Hambrick in the book *Strategic Leadership* (1996) "The replacement of one leader by another has been a matter of fascination and drama through the ages" (163). The passing of one leader and the succession of another with the questions of continuity or disruption, winners or losers, evokes the political metaphor in whatever type of organization it occurs. As outlined by Finkelstein and Hambrick (1996), executive succession generally follows a prescribed trajectory:

> At the start of the succession framework is the precipitating context, or the conditions that influence, and surround the departure of the predecessor. These contextual factors include: 1) the performance of the organization, 2) agency conditions (including ownership and board factors), 3) other organizational characteristics (such as size, structure, strategy), 4) external conditions, and 5) the characteristics of the predecessor (including background, tenure, power, and personality).
>
> This precipitating context, in turn, affects whether (or when) succession will occur and the process by which it will unfold - the succession event and process. Next, on the basis of the precipitating context and succession process, one is in a position to explain or understand the successor characteristics (e.g., insider versus outsider and similarity to predecessor).
>
> Finally, one can examine the effects of succession. Here, areas of interest include the successor's

behaviors, organizational changes, organizational performance, and the reaction of stakeholders (including investors). (p. 164)

This stage of the evolution of COGIC leadership again mirrors the typical case for an organization that began under a charismatic leader. This type of system has a built-in instability. The legitimacy of the command structure rests in the characteristics of one person and the commands themselves find unquestioned acceptance because of the belief in that one person's inspiration or gifts. Therefore, at the passing of the charismatic leader it is normal for these types of organizations to go through a period of uncertainty until it is decided which type of organization it will become. Consequently, when the charismatic leader dies the question of legitimate succession always arises. When the paramount (charismatic) authority is about to pass on it is typical (especially in political and religious movements) for the organization to splinter, with several leaders claiming to be the true heir. In addition, it is highly unlikely that a second charismatic leader will follow the founder and the organization thus begins immediately to lose its charismatic form. In such a case, it is normal for a charismatic organization to evolve into one of two types of successor organizations. If the succession follows a hereditary line, the organization becomes traditional in form. This means that tradition will be the guiding force in its continued development. And if the line of succession is determined by the application of an accepted set of rules the organization will begin to evolve down a bureaucratic line of growth (Morgan, 1997, p. 172-173; Pugh, Hickson, 1993, p. 4).

According to paragraph 2 of Article 7 of the COGIC constitution as amended December, 3, 1952, "Bishop C. H. Mason, the present Senior Bishop, shall retain his present power and authority during his life-time, but upon his death said authority shall revert to the Board of Bishops" (Pleas, 1991, p. 87). This provision gave clear direction as to the repository of power once Bishop Mason had passed from the scene. However, the Constitution (as it existed at the time of Mason's death) did not give any direction as to whether or not there should be a second Senior Bishop. In addition, it did not state if there was to be a continuation of this office. Nor did this constitution say if there was to be a second Senior Bishop what powers would he have or how the selection process should proceed.

According to S. P. Nesbitt, in his *The COGIC VOICE* (1965), for the first time in the history of the denomination the Board of Bishops was in complete and undisputed control of the Church (p.5). According to Patterson (1967) after Bishop Mason's death:

> According to the Constitution, the Church reverted to the Board of Bishops and the Board of Bishops jointly with the Board of State Bishops, then presided over by Bishop B. S. Lyles, retained the Executive Commission to have general supervision of the church for one year or until the National Convocation of 1962. (p. 1)

Nesbitt (1965) continues:

> At this juncture, there was no clear consensus as to what course to follow. Therefore, the Board decided to take additional time to discern what path the Church should pursue. The Commission petitioned the Board for a continuation of their authority so that they could continue the orderly administration of the denomination's business and to arrange for the selection of a successor to Bishop Mason. (p. 5; Joseph Williams, private conversation, July 15, 1999)

In response to this petition the Board of Bishops granted the seven men of the Commission the right to continue to function as a legitimate commission of the Church for one year, December 5, 1961 through December 5, 1962 (Nesbitt, 1965, p. 5; Cornelius, 1975, p. 79; Patterson, 1967, p. 1). Since these men had been directly involved in the administration of the Church with Bishop Mason it was believed this action would contribute to the continuity and stability of the denomination. The Board and the Assembly believed that at the end of this year the Commission (and any authority they had) would cease to exist, unless once again empowered by the Board of Bishops (Nesbitt, 1965, p. 5; Joseph Williams, private conversation, July 15, 1999). According to L. J. Cornelius in her book *Pioneer* (1975) it was at this time that the Commission began to be called the "Executive Board" (p. 79).

The current COGIC *Official Manual* states that the Special Commission "was authorized to make all appointments, execute other related business formerly performed by Bishop Mason" (COGIC, 1973, p. XXX) before the passing of the Senior Bishop. The *Official Manual* also quotes the 1926 Constitution, which stipulated that at the death of the founder:

> The leadership and supervision of the International Church would be reverted [sic] to the Board of Bishops with a directive to the General Assembly to elect, by a two-thirds vote of those present, two or more Bishops who will hold office, during good behavior, and shall have general supervision of the Church. The General Assembly, in keeping with this Constitutional provision, retained the seven men, elected five more members making a total of twelve. This twelve man Commission later changed its name to the Executive Board. (COGIC, 1973, p. XXXI)

This account, though "Official," makes no mention of the 1952 constitution, which was duly signed, sealed, registered and certified as a legal document on December 3, 1952 in the state of Tennessee (Pleas, 1991, p. 92). Moreover, it is very interesting that the 1926 constitution (as quoted in the current COGIC *Official Manual*) makes mention of the Commission when according to many sources it did not come into existence until the 1950s.

These two versions fairly represent the somewhat confused, almost dazed state of affairs in the Church of God in Christ almost one year after the death of their long-time charismatic leader. The flow of events moved inexorably toward a resolution. And so, as 1962 came to a close just as in every year since 1906, COGIC prepared to end the year with its greatest occasion, the Holy Convocation.

Within the Church of God in Christ, there is one institution, which has had an uninterrupted existence from the inception of the denomination until today. This institution is the Holy Convocation. Under Bishop Mason, Convocation was held annually from November 25 to December 14. As soon as he died, these dates and the length and format of the annual meeting began to change. Currently, the Holy Convocation is held from November 9 through November 16. Bishop Mason established the convocation and perpetuated it in a conscious effort to emulate and institutionalize the atmosphere of the Azusa Street Revival of 1906-1909. The convocation provided necessary "sacred time" for the socially and economically deprived members of America's largest African-American Pentecostal denomination (Turner, 1983, p. 147).

Bishop Clemmons expressed this vital period of renewal with the statement:

> Their strong African base and their marginal life
> in the United States motivated the early black holi-

ness-pentecostal founding fathers and mothers to link the spiritual and the temporal. The unique spirituality gave the Saints their own sense of reality. The gatherings were designed to ground the Saints in their unique identity. In racist America, the poor and the oppressed needed another sense of reality, not an escape from the historical marginalized existence but a transcendent sense that informed and gave meaning to the present. The convocation became a strengthening, transforming experience. (Clemmons, 1996, p. 75)

Under Bishop Mason's leadership, the Convocation traditionally began with three days and nights of fasting and prayer. This operated as the doorway from their normal existence into the sacred time and space. It also served some extremely vital services directed at the continuity of belief and practice. The Convocation provided a stage for the preservation of COGIC's oral history through the recitation of stories. Here younger people heard the stories of the fathers and mothers of the Church. Thus they received initiation into the understanding of what Mason and his co-laborers meant by Holiness (Clemmons, 1996, p. 73-80).

That the decision as to who would be the next Senior Bishop was expected by many people at the 1962 Convocation and that there had been pre-Convocation electioneering or positioning is reflected in an article that was published in the *Tri-State Defender* (November 24, 1962) on the day before the Convocation convened:

Who will be the next leader of the three-million member Church of God in Christ? That question will be decided by the delegates attending the 55th Holy Convocation here at Mason Temple between Nov. 25 and Dec 8. The newly elected leader will fill the vacancy created by the death of Bishop Charles Harrison Mason, founder of the church who died in Detroit last year on the eve of the 54th annual convocation. ... Among the strong contenders for the office are Bishop A. B. McEwen, pastor of the Lane Ave. Church of God in Christ, and O. T. Jones of Philadelphia, leader of the Youth Department who delivered the eulogy for the late leader. Bishop McEwen has been serving as the chairman of the specially appointed board of executive commissioners who have been directing the affairs of the church since they were named to the posts by the late Bishop Mason. Bishop Jones, who is reportedly the senior bishop in the church, in point of service, will be another strong contender for the top office. The leader of the Church's Youth Department, he was endorsed for the high office by delegates to the Youth Convention in Detroit last summer. His oldest son, Rev. O. T. Jones, Jr., told the assembled delegates that Bishop Jones was comparable to Joshua during the pilgrimage of the children of Israel after the death the leader, compared to Moses, should rightfully be elevated to the office. In preparation for the election, advance conferences have been held throughout the country to acquaint delegates with constitutional procedures of the church which govern the election. (p. 1-2; these events were also supported by Anonymous, personal communication, 1999)

As the 55th annual Holy Convocation came to a close in December of 1962, no one had been chosen to fill the office of Senior Bishop. It was therefore decided that the Board of Bishops needed to take appropriate action to fill the void and provide leadership for the Church. After an extended period of prayer, discussion and meditation it was decided that "a committee of twelve men would be set apart to act with the Board of Bishops in giving leadership to the Church UNTIL THE NEW SENIOR BISHOP COULD BE DULY ELECTED." (emphasis in the original) (Nesbitt, 1965, p. 5)

It was further decided that this 12-man Committee would be made up of the seven men from Bishop Mason's Committee, two men selected by the Elder's Council and three men selected by the Board of Bishops. The Board also chose the Chairman and Vice-chairman of the Committee, Bishop A. B. McEwen and Bishop J. S. Bailey respectively.

Bishop Patterson records this same event by saying:

> During the National Convocation of 1962 ... the Board of Bishops considered it wise to present the existing Executive Commission with an additional five men to the General Assembly for their election as *permanent* (emphasis added) executive officers of the Church. They also voted to change the name to Executive Board (or Executive Board of Bishops). (Patterson, 1967, p. 1)

This must have appeared to answer the question of leadership, or at least until the final hour of the Convocation. After the Board of Bishops chose the 12-men, one of the members of the Committee of 12 (Cornelius, 1975, p. 80), specifically Bishop J. O. Patterson (Anonymous, private conversation, October, 26, 1999) shared what he termed "a dream or vision that God had given him," in this dream or vision he said God had shown him that "Bishop O. T. Jones, Sr. was the man to lead the Church" (Nesbitt, 1965, p. 5). Another member of the Committee seconded Patterson's motion that Bishop Jones be elected. Then several other members of the Committee gave speeches, which indicated that they believed "God was moving by His Spirit"

(Cornelius, 1975, p. 80; Nesbitt, 1965, p. 5) in selecting Bishop Jones as the next COGIC Senior Bishop. This motion, to elect Bishop O. T. Jones, Sr. as the second Senior Bishop was voted upon and carried by a clear majority of the General Assembly. (Cornelius, 1975, p. 80; Nesbitt, 1965, p. 5)

One public source appears to back up this account (with a twist as to who presented the nomination) of Bishop Jones being "elected" to fill the position of Senior Bishop as it had existed under Bishop C. H. Mason. This source also reveals dimensions of the power struggle (DuBois, 1966, p. 8; Synan, 1986, p. 55; Thomas, 1966, p. 1) as it was reported to have developed within the Executive Board and is found in an article published in the *Tri-State Defender* (December 22, 1962):

> The son and [sic] founder of the Church of God in Christ, Elder C. H. Mason, Jr. is credited with sparking the election of Bishop O. T. Jones of Philadelphia, Pa., to the head of the international church which boasts of a five-million membership.
>
> Elder Mason, pastor of the first established church of that faith, Temple Church of God in Christ, 672 S. Lauderdale St., broke a 10-day deadlock over the election of a senior bishop of the church to *fill a vacancy created by the death of his father* (emphasis added) about a year ago. The executive board of the church which consists of 12 bishops had ended in a 10-day deadlock of debate on who should be *elected* (emphasis added) senior bishop, with "we will wait, until the 1963 Holy Convocation to elect the head of the church." ... Bishop McEwen of Memphis had been Bishop O. T. Jones greatest competitor for the position. The Convocation's general assembly for 1962 were standing to be dismissed when Elder

Mason requested of the chairman and was granted the floor. He made a passionate plea for the General Assembly to elect Bishop Jones as the head of the church before dismissal. As Elder Mason spoke forthrightly and soberly, the great assembly became deathly quiet and the delegates took their seats again. Mason said, while pointing to Bishop Jones "he is the last living of the first six bishops ordained in the Church of God in Christ. As such he is the unofficial senior bishop in terms of seniority." He continued, "Bishop Jones merits this honor," said Mason as he strongly urged the general assembly to elect him the head. The assembly of an estimated 5,000 crushed the silence with a burst of applause. Mason continued fervently, "The pioneer fathers of this church who have served faithfully sould [sic] be placed in positions of leadership and advice to the church," said Mason. He added: "I am a younger man who wants to look everybody in the eye and say that, if I'm elevated to a higher position in this church that I merited it ... not because I am the son of the late Bishop Mason, founder of the church, therefore I use short cuts to honorable positions." Comments from various delegates, during Mason's talk have [sic] strong indication that they agreed with his request. Bishop Jones was swept into office minutes before the assembly was adjourned. He is the second senior bishop of the church in its 60 years of existence. After the delegates were dismissed many were heard saying, "Elder Mason's stand for electing Bishop Jones as the senior bishop held our church together." ("Philadelphia minister," 1962)

Many of the statements used by the author of this article, such as, "As Elder Mason spoke," "Mason said, while pointing," "Comments from various delegates, during Mason's talk," and "After the delegates were dismissed many were heard saying," point to the author having been an eyewitness to these events.

Historical Recording Secretary L. J. Cornelius (1975) chronicled this same event by saying:

> One of the members of the Executive Board told a dream or vision which he had that indicated he saw Bishop Mason bringing Bishop O. T. Jones. Consequently others felt that Bishop Jones being one of the First Bishops appointed by Bishop Mason in the Church would be the most qualified from experience. Thus he was nominated and seconded by interesting speeches to make it clear that God was moving. The motion to elect Bishop Jones was put forth and carried by an over whelming majority of those present in the General Assembly. He was elected unaminously [sic]. (p. 80)

According to Patterson in his widely circulated booklet *Official* (1967), this same election proceeded as follows:

> After the General Assembly had finished the other business which had duly and properly come before it, Bishop McEwen called for a motion to adjourn. It was then that Bishop J. S. Bailey intercepted and proceeded to maneuver the house into position to entertain the motion that elected "Bishop" Jones to the honorary position of Senior Bishop. This was not Divine intervention to overthrow the Executive Board which had just a few minutes earlier been elected head of the Church as some would have you believe. This was a well calculated [sic] plan by members of the Executive Board them-

selves. Bishops J. S. Bailey, W. Wells, J. O. Patterson
and the late Elder C. H. Mason, Jr., and others had
looked upon the feeble condition of "Bishop" Jones
and also his seniority, and in the caucus meeting felt
that if they defined some way acceptable to the
General Assembly by which "Bishop" Jones could
be given the special honor, it would perhaps prolong
his life. After much discussion, Bishop Bailey
advanced the idea of the Methodist Church honoring
the oldest bishop with the title, "Senior Bishop."
Although he is only a member of the Board of
Bishops with one vote, he does receive ceremonial
honor. Bishop Wells made the following motion:

> That Bishop O. T. Jones be recognized or
> honored as the Senior Bishop of the Church and
> that Bishop A. B. McEwen's position as
> Chairman of the Executive Board would remain
> status quo, also that details of how these two offi-
> cers would function, would be worked out in the
> April, 1963 session. (p. 1)

Bishop W. A. Patterson wrote many articles and letters
that appeared in the *Whole Truth Magazine* during this time.
He was a participant and eyewitness to many of the meet-
ings, which were central to the process of choosing a new
leader. He recorded his impressions in the book *From the
Pen of Bishop W. A. Patterson* (1970). The process by which
Bishop O. T. Jones, Sr. became COGIC's second Senior
Bishop is recorded by Bishop W. A. Patterson under the title
"Who Tricked Whom In The 55th National and International
Convocation?" In this article, Bishop Patterson adds insight
into the behind-the-scenes meetings and adds support to var-
ious portions of the other variations of this event:

Let us begin in Chicago with the Committee of Seventeen which met to work out rules and a platform to offer to the Board of Bishops when we met in Memphis, Tennessee. They reported that they had a prayerful and peaceable meeting. There were members of the Commission who did not want the Committee to meet; but in spite of the opposition the Committee met.

The first day most of the articles were accepted; but on the second day, they tore up most of what they had agreed upon on the first day. The Chicago Instrument made all the ordained ministry, state mothers, district superintendents, district missionaries, state chairmen of various departments, eligible to vote; but on the second day this was destroyed, and after much discussion a certain one recommended that the State Bishop be elected by his State as the State delegate with one Pastor who could not vote unless the Bishop was not there. This scheme worked in most of the States, for the Pastors were afraid to vote otherwise. But when they went to Convocation and found that some of the God-fearing Bishops did not try to deprive the Pastors of the God-given right, this plan began to weaken.

The Bishops met to test their strength, and many of them wanted to carry their plans to the General Assembly and read it as an ultimatum; but when they saw that they did not have strength enough to do this, then they centered their attention on an Election and Balloting Committee. But after much differing, they compromised by merging the committees. And when these Committees got things almost worked out, a certain one said, "We do not have enough time to have an election, in this meeting." Bishop Ford offered a solution. He said that if the Commissioners would agree that Bishop A. B. McEwen be the No. 1 man, that Bishop Bailey be his Assistant, and Bishop J. O. Patterson be the Executive Secretary, this would work. But this struck fire and Bishop Bailey made the statement that "We do not have enough time to have an election in this meeting." Bishop McEwen, said, "We do, for people were told that we would elect a leader in this meeting."

By this time, it was known that if there was an election, Bishop McEwen would get it; for with the Bishop Bailey plan that the State Bishops be the delegates, there were fifty State Bishops signed up for Bishop McEwen the first week of the meeting, and this number grew to about sixty-seven. Someone got to Bishop McEwen and got him to ask the Bishops to wait and this is where he lost his chance. Bishop McEwen feeling secure said that he wanted all of the Commissioners to remain in office and to add five more which was another violation; for all the entire office expired December 6th, and all was to be voted on according to qualifications prescribed by the Committee.

A certain Bishop contended that we wait, and they voted to wait until April. They pacified the pastors by letting them elect three of the five men for the Executive Board, formerly known as the Board of Commissioners. The pastors elected three men: Bishops Shipman, Wells and Ford. The Bishops elected Bishop C. E. Bennett and Bishop John White. Now the men feeling that there would be no election until April began to leave for home - - But on the last day and about the last minute - - - !

Just before they could dismiss, Mother Coffey asked who should she look to; she felt she should have one person to look to. She did not know that she was asking a leading question.

Bishop McEwen was sitting confidently by to hear them declare him the head man, at least until April. But then the Master Plan began to be set in motion. Elder C. H. Mason, Jr., asked that Bishop Jones be given some special recognition. He told how Bishop Mason ordained the first five Bishops and all are dead but Bishop Jones, and since Bishop Jones was the first one Bishop Mason put his hands on, he is the Senior Bishop in the Church.

This was Bishop Bailey's cue. He then called for Bishop J. O. Patterson to talk. Bishop Patterson said, "I guess Bishop Bailey wants me to tell you what I told the Bishops about seeing Bishop Mason." Bishop Patterson said someone knocked at his door and that he said to Sister Alice, "That is no one but Reatha (another sister)." He told Sister Alice to let her in, then changed his mind and said, "I'll go." When he got to the door, Bishop Mason had already let himself in and had Bishop Jones by the hand and said to him, "Boy, what are your hands doing so cold?" This was to say to the Convocation or let them believe that Bishop Mason had come back from the dead and appointed Bishop Jones to lead the Church. Bishop Bailey said, "The Lord has spoken."

Remember, the Committee was told to not meet in Chicago; the Bishops were told that they should not meet in Memphis; the Counsil [sic] was told that there was not time enough to have an election in this meeting; but is now saying —- This is the time. Bishop Bailey was so eager to elect Bishop Jones, he attempted to take over the chairmanship, but one of the Bishops told him that he was out of order for he was not chairman of the meeting. They then called for Bishop D. L. Williams, the newly elected chair-

man of the Bishops Board —- the house that said
that "We will wait until April." Bishop Williams
came forth and put the motion. Many objected, but
the motion prevailed ... This group was so well organized until no one that opposed them was permitted
to speak. Many of the saints think that this was not a
prearranged plan; but you ask those that engineered
this plot, they may tell you. If not someone can.

As we come to the finishing line, let us consider
"Who tricked whom." The Committee of Seventeen
was tricked out of a well-planned instrument for
election. The Board of Bishops was tricked into letting the State Bishop to be the only delegate from his
State with one dummy pastor who could not vote.
This Board of Bishops that said the Church was in
the Board's hands was tricked by another group that
said, "We run this Church." Having outsmarted all
groups and with no other mountains to conquer, no
one else to trick, they then start on their own group.

First, Bishop McEwen, not knowing what was
going on behind his back, and feeling secure, makes
his appointments. He left Bishop Williams of
Wisconsin out in the cold; he left Bishop Mack E.
Jones of Ohio out in the cold; he left the Texas brothers dangling (but adjusted this matter later); he
appointed two State Bishops and sat down to let his
assistant close out.

Then comes the request for recognition for
Bishop Jones; then comes the dream, vision or whatever it was; then the motion and Bishop McEwen
was out, or dangling. Now, if you will remember
what you said: That Bishop Jones will be over the
spiritual side of the Church and Bishop McEwen
will be over the natural or temporal side; thereby
leaving Bishop McEwen, chairman of the Trustee

Board. Dear brothers, when you tricked Bishop McEwen, you tricked yourselves: for he is the chairman of your board, therefore, you made your Board a Trustee Board. (p. 4-8)

Another source that casts a light, almost as confusing as it is revealing upon the elevation of Bishop Jones to the position of COGIC's second Senior Bishop is an article printed in the *Tri-State Defender* (December 15, 1962):

Just one year after he delivered the eulogy for Bishop Charles H. Mason, founder and chief apostle of the Church of God in Christ, Bishop O. T. Jones of Philadelphia was *elected* (emphasis added) to head the church which boasts some three million members. The *election* (emphasis added) of Bishop Jones to the high post was considered the climax of the 55th Annual Convocation for the churches which convened at Mason Temple from Nov. 25 through Dec. 7. The name of the new *leader of the church* (emphasis added) was withheld from the public until the last day of the meeting and the information given out during a conference in the office of Bishop Lewis H. Ford, director of public relations and presiding bishop of the First Episcopal Diocese of Illinois of Churches of God in Christ. When Bishop Jones was *appointed* (emphasis added) to the high post, it ended speculation that the church which had been held together for more than half a century under the leadership of the late Charles Harrison Mason would be broken into fragments. A campaign to have Bishop Jones *appointed* (emphasis added) to the top post was started last summer in Detroit during a Youth Convention. Bishop A. B. McEwen was also a leading contender as chairman of the

Executive Commission which had directed the affairs of the church for more than a year. Bishop Jones is the oldest ordained bishop in the church and has served in the ministry for 50 years. ("Philadelphia minister," 1962)

The way this article switches between "elected" and "appointed" lends credence to the belief that there was contemporaneous confusion as to what actually happened at the end of the 1962 Holy Convocation with regard to how Bishop Jones became Senior Bishop without doing anything to help clear up that confusion. It also adds another dimension to the story of the mechanics of this event when it says, "The name of the new leader was withheld from the public until the last day of the meeting and the information was given out during a conference in the office of Bishop Lewis H. Ford, director of public relations" ("Philadelphia minister," 1962).

Here there is no mention of a last-minute nomination, no recounting of a prophetic dream, instead there is a clinical recital of a public press release. The reality of this staged press release is supported by a photograph that accompanies the article entitled "With New Church Leader" ("Philadelphia minister," 1962). In this photograph, Bishop O. T. Jones (who is seated in the center) is surrounded by Bishops A. B. McEwen, J. O. Patterson, L. H. Ford, J. White, W. Wells, J. S. Bailey, C. E. Bennett, and W. G. Shipman. The caption says, "Bishop O. T. Jones, center, was elected senior bishop of Churches of God in Christ, Inc. at a recent assembly held here in Memphis" ("Philadelphia minister, 1962").

These actions, however they proceeded, show a charismatic organization trying to find its way after the death of the founding charismatic leader, who brought the organization into being. Although there were direct appeals to the bureaucratic superstructure of rules and regulation, which Mason used as a framework for his creation, by the very act of choosing another Senior Bishop to succeed Bishop C. H. Mason when there was no written provision to do so, COGIC was beginning to proceed down a traditional organizational trajectory.

Looking to organizational theory for its prediction of such actions shows that the experience of COGIC provides a classic example of the routinization of charisma. Max Weber, the German Social Scientist who is the undisputed father of the organizational theories of charisma, describes certain means of choosing a successor to the original charismatic leader. When looking at the problem of choosing a successor, Weber states:

> These interests generally become conspicuously evident with the disappearance of the personal charismatic leader and the problem of succession, which inevitably arises. The way in which this problem is met, if it is met at all and the charismatic group continues to exist, is of crucial importance for the character of subsequent social relationships ... Designation of a successor by a charismatically qualified administrative staff and his recognition by the community. In its typical form this process should quite definitely not be interpreted as "election" or "nomination" or anything of the sort. It is not a matter of free selection, but one which is strictly bound to objective duty. It is not determined merely by majority vote, but is a question of the right person who is truly endowed with charisma. It is quite possible that the minority and not the majority should be right in such a case. Unanimity is often required. [And in what could only be called a prescient addition Weber continues] It is obligatory to

acknowledge a mistake and persistence in error is a serious offence. Making a wrong choice is a genuine wrong requiring expiation. (as quoted in Eisenstadt, 1968, p. 56)

Bishop Ozro Thurston Jones (1891-1972), the man elected to be the Church of God in Christ's second Senior Bishop, was born in Fort Smith, Arkansas. He confessed salvation in 1912. He immediately said that he experienced total sanctification, the baptism with the Holy Ghost and a call to the ministry. According to L. J. Cornelius (1975), "He pioneered along with Bishop Mason and helped trail blaze in greenfileds [sic] until men and women accepted this great truth of Holiness" (p. 80). Elder Jones was appointed by Chief Apostle Mason in 1914 as the first leader of COGIC's National Youth Department. In this position he founded the Young People Willing Workers (YPWW), the National COGIC Youth Congress, and *Quarterly Topics* youth magazine (*The Whole Truth,* Spring, 1996, p. 13; Cornelius, 1975, p. 80; Mason, 1991, p. 30; Nesbitt, 1965, p. 7-8; Pleas, 1991, p. 23).

Jones first gained widespread recognition for his dynamic preaching while holding integrated revivals in Coffeeville, Kansas as early as 1917. He "preached out" (founded through evangelistic revival meetings; cf. White, 1969, p. 146-147) and organized 18 churches in Arkansas, Kansas, and Oklahoma (Cornelius, 1975, p. 80; Weeks, 1989, p. 11). This earned him an appointment as Assistant Overseer of the state of Oklahoma. After several years in this post, Mason sent him to pastor a small church in Pennsylvania. Within a year, Mason appointed Jones to be the Overseer of Pennsylvania. Under his leadership, Jones' church grew to over 400 families while the state jurisdiction grew from only 11 churches to more than 200. During this time Jones also helped to organize COGIC's work in

Pennsylvania, Delaware, Maryland and the District of Columbia serving for a time as the Overseer of these areas.

Nineteen twenty-eight, marked the birth of the National Youth Congress, which Jones established as the second largest annual gathering of the Church (after the Holy Convocation). Which, according to the *Whole Truth* (Spring, 1996) "was at one time the largest convention for African-American youth in North America" (p. 13). In 1933 Senior Bishop Mason consecrated Jones as one of the first five original COGIC Bishops and was considered the first in order of these five (Mason, 1991, p. 28-30; Weeks, 1989, p. 11; Woolfolk, 1997, p. 5).

By the time he was elected to be COGIC's second Senior Bishop, O. T. Jones, Sr. had been an ordained minister in the Church for 50 years. In addition to the foregoing brief outline of Bishop Jones' long and distinguished career, he also served the Church as President of the National Board of Education, Trustee of the original Corporation of the Church of God in Christ, member of Bishop Mason's Commission, and co-author of the first *Official Manual* of the Church of God in Christ. One indication of the importance and renown of Bishop Jones' ministry in the years just prior to his election as Senior Bishop is reflected in the fact that he addressed the Pentecostal World Congress held in Toronto in 1958 (Nesbitt, 1965, p. 7-8; Burgess, et al. 1988, p. 512).

In 1963, when he presided for the first time as Senior Bishop at the Holy Convocation, the divinely ordained aspect of his election, as well as the support of the next generation of COGIC leaders, for Bishop Jones was vividly exposed. This occurred when various leaders vocally supported him before the Convocation expressing the belief that he was the man chosen by God to fill the office of Senior Bishop and urging all to follow him loyally into the future. This scene is recorded by eyewitness L. J. Cornelius (1975):

Many Bishops and Workers stood on the platform and highly commended our Bishop Jones and
pledged their loyalty to him. Mother Coffey stood
and declared her fidelity to him and begged the
bretheren [sic] to stand by and work with Bishop
Jones in her Motherly authoritive [sic] manner rec-
ommending him as a God sent Leader. Bishop
Wyoming Wells told how he was saved under him
and trained by him and would ever be loyal to him.
Bishop Samuel Crouch, Bishop O. M. Kelly and
Bishop Mack Jonah spoke highly of his leadership
and counted him worthy of the new position he was
elected to as Senior Bishop. Many of the Bishops
and State Mothers spoke honoring him. The old pioneers that had worked with him through the years
blessed him. (P. 80)

Since the line of succession was determined not by the
application of a written set of rules for the organization but
by the tradition of having a Senior Bishop, its continued
evolution can be seen as proceeding down a traditional trajectory (Morgan, 1997, p. 172-173; Pugh, Hickson, 1993, p.
4; Weber as cited in Eisenstadt, 1968, p. 54-56). This situation was complicated by the fact that once he was installed
as the Senior Bishop, Bishop Jones acted as if the Church
was instead following a bureaucratic trajectory by con-
stantly referring to the written rules of the Church as the
foundation of authority (e.g., the "Rules and Regulations
Are Needed" section of Jones' leadership Digest in
Nesbitt's *The COGIC VOICE*, 1965, p. 9). This divergence
between what type of organization the Church's actions typified (traditional) and what type it was projected and perceived to be (bureaucratic) pointed the way toward future
problems. This situation was further aggravated because at
the same time Bishop Jones personal style of leadership was

autocratic (e.g. the numerous appointments and independent actions chronicled in Nesbitt's *The COGIC VOICE*, 1965). An examination of Bishop Jones' view of the type of organization the Church constituted, as well as his personal philosophy of leadership, strengthens this determination.

The examination into Bishop Jones' view on these subjects looks at two foundational statements, which he released, that either directly or indirectly addressed the two conditions, leadership style and organizational type. The first is eight things in which Bishop Jones said he believed, and the second is a statement he made about giving leadership to the Church (as chronicled by S. P. Nesbitt). Two verbatim quotes from the Bishop himself highlight these areas. The first of these quotes is:

Things which I believe:

I believe in a Church where Law and Order are respected and followed.

I believe in equality for all – if not, we should close the doors of the Church.

I believe in a Church where women and men are given an opportunity to express themselves to the limit of the ability which God gives them.

I believe in a Church which is guided by the Spirit of God in which the Holy Scriptures serve as the basis for faith and practice.

I believe in a Church where State Bishops preside over their states without interference from National Officers.

I believe in a Church which conducts its affairs in accordance with the highest possible standards of efficiency, responsibility and accountability – I shall seek, by the help of God, to effect better policies governing the business operations of the Church.

I believe in a Church where pastors should have

the freedom to pastor their churches without fear, but also in which pastors respect the leadership which appoints them.

I believe in a Ministry which is above moral reproach and which is directed and sustained by the Holy Ghost. (Nesbitt, 1965, p. 8)

It is clear from the above quote that Bishop Jones believed in the rule of "Law and Order" (Nesbitt, 1965, p. 8). He viewed his own succession to the office of Senior Bishop as the result of the application of the accepted set of rules for the organization (even though there was no written provision for a second Senior Bishop). He also considered his administration to flow from the implementation of those same rules (Nesbitt, 1965, p. 8). The evolution of the organization as projected by this new leader would therefore have proceeded into bureaucratic forms (Morgan, 1997, p. 172-173; Pugh, Hickson, 1993, p. 4) while in contravention to this projected view the organization was actually adhering to traditional forms through a charismatic office (Eisenstadt, 1968, p. 57; Morgan, 1997, p. 172; Pugh, Hickson, 1993, p. 4).

The second of these quotes is entitled:

Digest of the Senior Bishop's Approach to Giving Leadership to the Church.

DO FIRST THINGS FIRST

Before we can know what needs to be done, it is necessary that investigation be made to ascertain the facts in the case before us. Diagnosis can come only after we have had time to conduct a thorough examination of all phases of our Church's operation. When we know what our condition is, we will be able to prescribe the course of action which we will follow. Accordingly:

"The Senior Bishop will select and appoint several committees of qualified persons made up of representatives of every part of the Church to make a thorough study of our ENTIRE NATIONAL WORK.

The COMMITTEES that will be appointed will make a study of the following areas, and make recommendations concerning the same: namely,

1. A Committee for making a complete survey of all our property at our Church Headquarters.
2. A Committee for making a complete survey of all our Church's Finances and Financial System.
3. A Committee for making a complete survey of all our Church's Publications.
4. A Committee for making a complete survey of all our Church's Departments and Auxiliaries.

After these reports have been received and studied, a Report will be made to the GENERAL ASSEMBLY, so that the entire Church may be able to study the reports, and recommend whatever action on them the GENERAL ASSEMBLY may deem proper and necessary."

LEADER MUST SERVE THE PEOPLE FAITHFULLY AND JUSTLY –
Accordingly,

"It is my intention to give FULL-TIME to the work of the SENIOR BISHOP.

It is my determination, by the help of God, to do nothing but what is right.

Above all, the Word of God shall be my rule for Faith and Practice,"

"Be ye followers of me, even as I also am of Christ. " (I Corinthians 11:1)

RIGHTEOUS COUNSEL IS ALWAYS NEDED

"Where no counsel is, the people fall; but in the multitude of counselors there is safety." (Proverbs 11:14)

Accordingly, "I have appointed a Board of Special Advisors To The Senior Bishop, and other appropriate committees to give advice and counsel."

RULES AND REGULATIONS ARE NEEDED

"Having been the one commissioned by our late Senior Bishop, Bishop C. H. Mason, to clarify and codify our Church's doctrines and practices, I am fully aware of the contents of our existing Constitution, and of our existing Constitutional needs at this time.

Therefore, as Senior Bishop, I will do all that is in my power to see to it that the Church is presented with recommendations of those rules and regulations which seem necessary for the continued spiritual and material growth of our Church.

However, whatever finally is done in this regard, in order for it to be right, must be done according to the basic scriptural structure of our Church, and be done through the existing arteries of the Church.

Moreover, the committee that shall be appointed to make a study and recommendations to the GENERAL ASSEMBLY in this matter, will be made up of representatives of every segment of our Church.

> The proper rights and responsibilities of EVERY segment of our Church will be made clear and safe-guarded [sic].
>
> I ask your patience with us until, by the help of God, these matters can be worked out peacefully and according to the Word of God." (Nesbitt, 1965, p. 9)

The foregoing "Digest" reveals much about Bishop Jones' leadership style.

Initially, successors rely heavily upon the legitimacy of their position to take charge of their organization. If they want to become leaders as opposed to managers they must extend their power bases. This is usually accomplished through the implementation of three distinct strategies. First, they must learn about the organization. Even if they have been a long-time, upper-level subordinate there are perspectives about any organization that are only available to the paramount leader. Therefore, successors set out to learn about the organizational culture at the time of their ascension through the acquisition of technical knowledge useful in diagnosing problems and understanding issues. Secondly, successors work to build a coherent set of shared expectations between themselves and their followers. They strive to settle conflicts and to gather an effective team through appointments to key positions. Lastly, they must work to develop good working relationships with leaders from the past administration who might still hold key positions of power (e.g., board members, department heads) (Hackman & Johnson, 1996, p. 217-219). As reflected in the actions he took during the initial transition phase of his leadership, after his election as Senior Bishop, Bishop O. T. Jones, Sr. followed this type of a succession pattern.

Heckscher and Donnellon in *The Post-Bureaucratic*

Organization (1994) contend that "Organizations control on the basis of knowledge" (p. 118). When Bishop Jones stated the first order of business for his new administration would be, that "Investigations be made to ascertain facts in the case before us" (Nesbitt, 1965, p. 9), he made it clear that he intuitively understood this principle. Consequently, it appeared that he wanted what Heckscher and Donnellon (1994), referred to as "a store of documentary material ... maintained in order both to interact with the external environment and to control the functioning of the organization itself" (p. 118).

Although the rest of the "Digest" speaks eloquently of "Committees and Advisors" (Nesbitt, 1965, p. 9), this document outlines the nascent administration of an authoritarian, top-down leader within a developing bureaucratic environment. This is made clear in such statements as:

The Senior Bishop will *select and appoint* (emphasis added) several committees of *qualified* (emphasis added) persons ... The committees will be *appointed* (emphasis added) ... I have *appointed* (emphasis added) a Board of Special Advisors to the Senior Bishop, and other appropriate committees to give *advice and counsel* (emphasis added) ... *rules and regulations are needed* (emphasis added) ... However, whatever finally is done in this regard, in order for it to be right, must be done according to the Word of God, and according to the basic scriptural structure of the Church, *and be done through the existing arteries of the Church.* (emphasis added) (Nesbitt, 1965, p. 9)

The recurring and heavy accent on appointments to key committees by the Senior Bishop as opposed to elections by the General Assembly or the Board of Bishops reveals Bishop Jones' conception of the position of Senior Bishop as one of autocratic power — one where the Senior Bishop was not only free, but empowered to choose the personnel for the most important and sensitive structures in the Church without any check or balance by a wider authority. His style of leadership exemplified the type that Morgan (1997) describes as "Autocracy: absolute government where power is held by an individual or small group and supported by control of critical resources, property or ownership rights, tradition, charisma, and other claims to personal privilege" (p. 157).

Conversely, this document also shows that Bishop Jones projected the image of the Church organizationally as a bureaucracy, which is defined by Morgan as "rule exercised through the use of the written word, which provides the basis for a rational-legal type authority or 'rule of law'" (p. 157). Yet his own succession to the office of Senior Bishop was clearly outside the bounds of written rules and regulations and well within the expected actions of a traditional organization.

This conflict between how the organization was operating and how it was perceived and projected to operate set the stage for a confrontation between those who were adept at bureaucratic maneuver and those who wanted to gain power through tradition and rule by law. The seriousness of this dichotomy of action and projection was further complicated by the mismatch of an unfettered autocratic leader within what he perceived as a bureaucratic organization. These dislocations between action, perception and projection provided the seedbed of turmoil.

CHAPTER V
Bishop Jones' Tenure

Bishop O. T. Jones, Sr. was the undisputed leader of COGIC from December 1962 when he was elected Senior Bishop by the General Assembly until December 31, 1964 when a circular letter began to travel through the denomination, which called for a general meeting "without any prior notice to, consultation with, or authorization from the Senior Bishop" (Nesbitt, p. 19).

As the "second elected Senior Bishop" (Hall, 1995, p. 18), Bishop O. T. Jones, Sr. was a "vigorous and innovative executive" (Weeks, 1989, p.11) who "led the church during a difficult period" (Clemmons, 1996, p. 126) when "the church struggled to transcend the ordeals of transition (Clemmons, 1996, p. 126). "His patient and kind demeanor was an instrument of peace which helped us through a period when a steady hand was needed at the helm" (Hall, 1995, p.18). Cornelius (1975) ascribes Jones' vitality to divine intervention when she states, "Bishop Jones was not too well at the time of the Election but upon realizing he had been chosen he regained Faith and received new strength for the task of leading the Church" (p. 80). Mother Lillian Brooks Coffey, the National and International Supervisor of the Women's Department, is quoted by L. J. Cornelius in a section entitled, "A Tribute to the memory of our Founder, Bishop C. H. Mason" (Cornelius, 1975, p. 25) as saying in regard to Bishop Jones, "Now that we have another Senior Bishop, let's respect him, love, *obey and follow* (emphasis added) him! We all know him. He is a good man worthy of the promotion" (Cornelius, 1975, p. 26) showing that she did not perceive Bishop O. T. Jones, Sr. as merely a figurehead but instead as the fully empowered successor to Bishop C. H. Mason.

During the two years that Bishop Jones was the undisputed leader of COGIC, he devoted himself "Full-time to the work of Senior Bishop" (Nesbitt, 1965, p. 9; Cornelius, 1975, p. 80). While in this undisputed leadership Bishop Jones accomplished many things. He made several important appointments. He appointed bishops (Nesbitt, 1965, p. 11; Cornelius, 1975, p. 80); a new National Supervisor of the Women's Department (Nesbitt, 1965, p. 14); and a National President of the Youth Department (Nesbitt, 1965, p. 13; Fidler, 1964, p. 3; Cornelius, 1975, p. 80). He also established seven national study committees and appointed the chairmen and members of each (Nesbitt, 1965, p. 18). As Senior Bishop, Bishop Jones conducted an official census of the church in 1964 which reported 425,000 members in 4,100 congregations (Synan, 1986, p. 55). During this time the last home of Bishop Mason was purchased and dedicated as a shrine (Nesbitt, 1965, p. 12). Bishop Jones also tried to advance the cause of education and the first contacts were made with International Theological Center of the University of Georgia in Atlanta to explore the possibility of founding the C. H. Mason Theological Seminary as an affiliated school (Nesbitt, 1965, p. 13). Under Bishop Jones' administration the Home & Foreign Missions Department was active in spreading the gospel of Jesus Christ in 42 foreign nations and two US territories (Fidler, 1964, p. 12). As the undisputed leader and Senior Bishop Jones presided over two Holy Convocations- the 56th and the 57th (Nesbitt, 1965, p. 18; Cornelius, 1975, p. 80).

Two contemporaneous articles from local papers add credence to both sides in the "power struggle" (DuBois, 1966, p. 8; Synan, 1986, p. 55; Thomas, 1966, p. 1) that was about to engulf COGIC's organizational structure. Both articles clearly show Bishop O. T. Jones as the undisputed

Senior Bishop as evidenced by the fact that he is accorded an Official Day. And yet both articles show the Executive Board prominently conducting the business of the denomination. Both articles ran in the *Tri-State Defender.* The first article (November 30, 1963) stated:

Under a rallying banner of "unity" the 56th Holy Convocation of the Church of God in Christ will convene at Mason Temple, 958 S. Mason St., Nov. 25 to Dec. 6. This meeting will mark the first Holy Convocation of the Church of God in Christ *since Bishop O. T. Jones, of Philadelphia, Pa., was elected senior bishop* (emphasis added) of the church *with a 12-member Board of Executive Commissioners, headed by Bishop A. B. McEwen of Memphis* (emphasis added). Bishop Jones and Bishop McEwen *were elected* (emphasis added) in Dec., 1962, after the death of Bishop C. H. Mason, founder and organizer of the Church of God in Christ ... The day and night meeting will open with three days of fasting and prayer and climaxing Sunday, Dec. 1, *Official Day, when Bishop Jones will speak* (emphasis added) ... *Hosts to the Convocation are Bishop A. B. McEwen and Bishop J. O. Patterson of Memphis.* (emphasis added) ("Church of God in Christ's," 1963)

The second article (December 19, 1962) adds to the confusion by again showing Bishop O. T. Jones being honored with an Official Day but also showing the Executive Board conducting business. This article states:

The convocation officially opened with three days of fasting and prayer conducted by *Senior Bishop O. T. Jones* (emphasis added) who was *assisted by Bishops A. B. McEwen, chairman of the executive board and J. O. Patterson, general secretary* (emphasis added) ... On *"Official Day" Bishop Jones spoke* (emphasis added) on the subject of the "Christian Faith Only in Christ" ... *Business affairs of the church are carried on by an executive board.*

(emphasis added) ("10,000 Delegates," 1964)

Another aspect of this article that displays the confusion as to where the authority resided in the Church is shown in a picture that accompanied it. In this picture Mother Annie L. Bailey is shown being consecrated as the new National Supervisor of the Women's Department. Both Bishop Jones and the Executive Board are pictured as having been involved in the consecration.

CHAPTER VI

The Circular Letters and Accusations Against Bishop Jones

Having been legally elected and installed as the Senior Bishop of the Church of God in Christ (Cornelius, 1975, p. 80; Nesbitt, 1965, p. 5; Patterson, 1967, p. 1), what was the cause of the turmoil that engulfed and eventually ended his administration? In the words of one GOGIC pastor that I interviewed:

Everyone loved Dad Mason, everyone honored and respected him. He could do things no other person could ever do. No one ever questioned his authority, his motives, or his decisions. And when Bishop Jones took over as Senior Bishop he thought that he could run things the same way. But he wasn't Dad and there were people who thought they had just as much right to run things as Jones did. And so after a while they did what they had to gain power. (J. Williams, personal communication, July 15, 1999)

This may have reflected the feelings of many, but formal action and specific allegations, which followed a bureaucratic logic, were advanced (Nesbitt, 1965, p. 26-28; Patterson, 1969, p. 15; Tennessee v. Jones, 1966). Some members of the leadership saw this as a war for organizational power as evidenced by the statement, "The question of 'Where the authority of the Church of God in Christ is placed by its Constitution?' was the issue that sparked the war" (Patterson, et, al., 1969, p. 77). Or as L. J. Cornelius (1975) described it:

87

Letters began to be sent all over the brethern [sic] territory stating conditions had to be changed. No one man would ever again run the church, no one but Bishop Mason could have that priviledge [sic]. Meetings were called by the Executive Board in an effort to gain control of the Church. Meetings were called by the Bishop and his cabinet to retain control. People were confused as to who to hear. Who is in charge of things [in Memphis]? The Executive Board was determined to see that Bishop O. T. Jones and his helpers, Bishop R. E. Ranger and his son, O. T. Jones, Jr. would not have the authority of the Church so it began to get worse and worse. (p. 81)

On December 31, 1965, the General Secretary of the Church of God in Christ, Bishop J. O. Patterson (1912-1989), who was also the son-in-law of the late Bishop C. H. Mason (Burgess, et al., 1988, p. 664), "extended a general invitation to the CHURCH OF GOD IN CHRIST MINISTERS AND LAYMEN FOR PROGRESS, to meet in Memphis, Tennessee, at 12:00 noon, February 3, 1965, at 229 South Wellington Street" (Nesbitt, 1965, p. 19; Patterson, 1967, p. 4-6). The first reason advanced for this meeting was to arrange for building maintenance such as, "water leaks, building needing painting and general repairs" (Nesbitt, 1965, p. 19; Patterson, 1967, p. 4-5, 13).

This first circular letter by the General Secretary evoked a response from Senior Bishop Jones in the form of another circular letter to the whole Church. In this January 11 response, Bishop Jones "stated that the extra meeting called by the General Secretary to the general Church was not properly authorized and therefore completely out of order" (Nesbitt, 1965, p. 19; Patterson, 1967, p. 7). Furthermore, the Bishop stated that no Executive or Board of the Church had asked him as Senior Bishop to call such a meeting. He also pointed out that unauthorized meetings would inevitably cause disruption to the unity of the Church. Bishop Jones reminded the Church that he had already taken measures to compile complete reports detailing the obligations, receipts, disbursements and transactions of the national organization and that these reports were scheduled to be presented to the Church at the Spring Call Meeting in April 1965 (Nesbitt, 1965, p. 19; Patterson, 1967, p. 7).

After receiving the Bishop's response, the General Secretary reiterated his call to the whole Church for a special meeting in a second circular letter. Bishop Patterson stated that he was calling the special meeting "with the authorization of the Executive Board" (Nesbitt, 1965, p. 20; Patterson, 1967, p. 10). In addition, he stated, "Senior Bishops are not an elective office, one becomes that by status of being. Actually after the passing of Bishop C. H. Mason there is definitely NO AUTHORITY vested in Senior Bishops" (Nesbitt, 1965, p. 20; Patterson, 1967, p. 8).

The General Secretary also included a copy of a resolution passed by the Executive Board. This resolution declared the office of Senior Bishop as the administrative and spiritual head of the Church no longer existed. It also contended that the office of Senior Bishop was not in reality an office but actually existed only as a ceremonial title used to refer to the bishop who was oldest in age or first in seniority of consecration. The resolution further stated that the appointive authority previously exercised by Bishop Mason now resided in the Executive Board (Nesbitt, 1965, p. 20; Patterson, 1967, p. 8-10).

After this second circular letter by the General Secretary the situation was further exacerbated by a circular letter sent to the whole Church on the letterhead of the "Co-Chairman of the International Executive Board" dated January 20, 1965 (Nesbitt, 1965, p. 20; Patterson, 1967, p. 12), Bishop J. S. Bailey (Patterson, 1967, p. 12; Patterson, et al., 1969, p.

77). The Co-Chairman addressed this letter "Dear Bishop and Fellow-worker" (Patterson, 1967, p. 12) but it was directed to the entire Church leadership. This is seen in the statement "Be sure to inform your Pastors and Ministers and stress to them the importance of their being present with you for your moral support, your support back home" (Patterson, 1967, p. 12). And it carried an implied threat or warning when it finished this admonishment by saying, "and for their own welfare Churchwise [sic]" (Patterson, 1967, p. 12). Above all else this letter echoed Bishop Patterson's call for the Special Meeting in Memphis on February 3-4, 1965. Bishop Bailey mentioned the circular letter that had been sent out by Bishop Jones as the reason for Bishop Patterson's second letter and joined that letter in urging people to "come without fail to this very important Meeting set for February 3 & 4th" (Nesbitt, 1965, p. 20). The actual reprint of the letter that Bishop Patterson includes in his *Official* (1967) aptly expresses the emphasis and urgency the Co-Chairman expressed, **"THIS IS YOUR CHURCH! YOU MUST COME AND HELP KEEP IT FROM GOING TO PIECES. I AM URGING YOU AND BEGGING YOU TO COME WITHOUT FAIL!"** (emphasis in the original) (p.12)

This letter was followed by a another circular letter sent out by the Chairman of the Board of Bishops, Bishop D. Lawrence Williams (Nesbitt, 1965, p. 6). In his letter Bishop Williams continued the confusion of bureaucratic and traditional organizational forms when he asked everyone in the Church "to loyally support our honorable and beloved Senior Bishop, Bishop O. T. Jones, in his endeavor to maintain and to continue *sound principles of governing* (emphasis added) the Church *as initiated by our late Bishop C. H. Mason* (emphasis added)" (Nesbitt, 1965, p. 20). He continued to use the language of bureaucracy when he also stated that "the Senior Bishop has requested a full and complete report from all departments of the General church for the Executive Conference scheduled to convene in Memphis, April 13-15, 1965" (Nesbitt, 1965, p. 20). In addition, Bishop Williams stated that "The meeting called by the General Secretary, February 2-3, 1965 has not been properly authorized" (Nesbitt, 1965, p. 20). Interestingly, Bishop Patterson makes no mention of this church-wide circular letter in his 1967 release, *Official.*

The day after the Chairman of the Board of Bishops sent his letter the General Secretary issued another circular letter calling for the special meeting to convene in February. This letter also used the language of bureaucracy (specifically the rational-legal authority mechanism of position see Morgan, *Images of Organization*, 1997, p. 172) to attack the legitimacy of the Chairman of the Board of Bishops. Bishop Patterson stated that the Chairman of the Board of Bishops was "wrong when he referred to himself as such; for ... the Board of Bishops has not elected a successor to its former Chairman who had been pressed not to return to the position of Chairman" (Nesbitt, 1965, p. 20). The General Secretary also alleged that the Chairman of the Board of Bishops was "wrong when he stated that the extra Meeting called by the General Secretary has not been duly and properly authorized" (Nesbitt, 1965, p. 20). Bishop Patterson concluded by asserting that "the vast majority of the Bishops and Pastors plan to attend [the February meeting] and have already made hotel reservations" (Nesbitt, 1965, p. 20). Just as the circular letter from Bishop D. Lawrence Williams was omitted by Bishop Patterson in his 1967 release *Official* neither is his response to this letter (which was also circulated to the whole Church) mentioned in this booklet.

In reference to the charge that Bishop Williams was not elected to the position of Chairman of the Board of Bishops and therefore not a holder of legitimate power it should be noted that Bishop Williams was elected Chairman of the

Board of Bishops on December 5, 1963. This action was taken through the adoption of a joint motion to accept the offered resignation of Bishop B. S. Lyle (the preceding Chairman) and to elect Bishop Williams as his successor. This motion was presented by Bishop J. W. Easter and seconded by Bishop P. J. Henderson (Nesbitt, 1965, p. 22).

According to Samuel P. Nesbitt in his publication *The COGIC VOICE*, the special call meeting of February 1969 produced a document that continued the appeal to bureaucratic rules and regulation. The General Secretary had this document delivered to the Senior Bishop "on or about February 8, 1965" (Nesbitt, 1965, p. 20). This document, issued by the General Secretary and the Executive Board Church of God in Christ, Inc. notified the Senior Bishop of the following allegations:

- that under the constitution and by-laws of the Church of God in Christ, there is no provision whatsoever for a Senior Bishop after the death of the late revered Bishop C. H. Mason;
- that the constitution and by-laws expressly state that on the death of Bishop Mason, the power, authority and government of the Church shall be vested in the Executive Board.
- that this Board was created by the late Bishop C. H. Mason.
- that its power and authority was recognized and ratified by the General Assembly ... on several occasions.
- that Bishop O. T. Jones has since 1962, usurped the power of the Executive Board, and abrogated unto himself the authority to appoint Bishops, Overseers and other Officials of the Church.
- that all the Senior Bishop's Appointments of State Bishops and National Officers were unlaw-

ful and without authority.
- that the Executive Board was making the appointments of six state Bishops and two National Officers who had been previously appointed by the Senior Bishop.
- that the Senior Bishop was being officially notified to cease and desist from making appointments as Senior Bishop.
- that from and after this time, the Executive Board will NOT recognize appointments made by the Senior Bishop, and we also serve notice that he nor any appointee he may name will act at their own risk and peril. (Nesbitt, 1965, p. 20)

The several references to the constitution and by-laws of the Church of God in Christ expose the bureaucratic basis of the allegations. The direct assaults on the administrative and appointive power of the Senior Bishop reflects the assertion that "Bishop O. T. Jones, Sr. was honored as the *Ceremonial* (emphasis added) Head of the Church with the title of 'Senior Bishop'" (Patterson, 1967, p. 1; Patterson, et al., 1969, p. 77). This reflection referred to the dichotomy between the traditional descent of Jones' position and power and the bureaucratic form he projected of the Church.

Making no reference to the document issued after the February 1965 meeting Bishop J. O. Patterson, in his booklet *Official* (1967), sums up this meeting and provides some collateral evidence that the state of repair at the National Headquarters was part of the original concerns of the General Secretary in calling this meeting. He does this in a section of the booklet headed by a question:

WHAT WAS THE OUTCOME OF THE SPECIAL CALL MEETING OF FEBRUARY 3, 1965?

It was a tremendous success. It was attended by more than fifty bishops, several hundred pastors and some laymen. The assembled body re-affirmed its allegiance to the Executive Board and demanded that the Executive Board perform its duties as executive head having general supervision of the Church. As a result of this meeting a new roof was put on Mason Temple at a cost of more than four thousand dollars and other bills and major repairs were cleared away on our national property. (p. 13)

Bishop Patterson, in his booklet *Official* (1967) continues his summation of the situation as it existed after the February 1965 meeting with an emotional section titled in bold caps:

WHAT DID THE SUPPORTERS OF "BISHOP" JONES DO WHEN IT BECAME OBVIOUS THAT THE CHURCH WAS NOT GOING TO ALLOW THEM UNDER THE GUISE OF "SENIOR BISHOP" TO DEPOSE THE EXECUTIVE BOARD AND TAKE THE LEADERSHIP OF THE CHURCH BY FORCE? (p. 13)

Under this heading Bishop Patterson states that Bishop Jones' supporters:

Began a smear campaign degrading the Executive Board, indicating their character and morals. They circulated throughout the brotherhood all kinds of defaming literature calling the Executive Board members liars, thieves, golfers, "Haman." They were accused of burning the home of the late Bishop Mason and also accused by implication of murdering his son, the late C. H. Mason, Jr. The Executive Board was accused by the opposition of misappropriating the Church's money and "fattening ourselves at the expense of the poor." (Patterson, 1967, p. 13)

The response of the Senior Bishop to the special meeting of February 1969 was issued on February 18, 1965 in another circular letter to the whole Church. In this letter Bishop Jones stated:

- that the General Secretary in a circular letter written over his signature as General Secretary, had called the entire Church to an extra meeting at the same time and place to the Meeting alleged in the Document to be a duly called Meeting of the Executive Board Church of God in Christ, Inc.
- that this Meeting was not properly authorized, and that due notice was not properly authorized was given to the entire Church by the Senior Bishop and the Chairman of the Board of Bishops.
- that no actions or directives attempted by any person or group at any improperly authorized Meeting can be considered law and order for the Church, and thus such actions may be disregarded.
- that, in the Church of God in Christ, the *General Assembly is the only doctrine-expressing and law-making body of the Church.*
- that if any person or group is permitted, at will to call unauthorized meetings and attempt to enact laws which could be binding upon the entire Church, then we would be permitting a direct

violation of the spirit of our Church and of a fundamental principle of our Constitution.

- that, should the Church condone such improper procedure. It would be permitting to come into existence a pattern of conduct which may destroy our existence as an organized body.
- that the attack made in this Document is not only upon the person and office of the Senior Bishop; but it is also a blatant disregard for the authority given by our Constitution to the *Board of Bishops* and to the *General Assembly.*
- that if this type of flagrant, *irresponsible procedure* becomes our pattern, then no one's position in the Church is secure;
- that, moreover, the attempted actions set forth in this Document present radical departure from the pattern (Heb. 8:5) which the Lord has revealed for order and government of our Church, and which - up until now - has served so well; [this is a direct appeal to tradition as a source of organizational procedure]
- that as Senior Bishop, he is deeply saddened that a circular letter from him was necessary; that he would have preferred to have worked to resolve between ourselves whatever difference may have existed;
- that, as Senior Bishop, his *sole* concern is for what is right in the sight of God.
- that therefore he is requesting the prayers of all for the Church and for himself the one whom the Lord has chosen to serve in the office of Senior Bishop, that we may ever abide in the unity of the Spirit and in the bonds of peace [an appeal to the charisma of divine appointment]. (Nesbitt, 1965, p. 21)

Besides the foregoing personal defense and the circular letter sent out by the Chairman of the Board of Bishops in support of Bishop Jones, Samuel P. Nesbitt of the Church of God in Christ Western Florida, Inc. published and mailed out a publication, *The COGIC Voice* (S. P. Nesbitt, personal communication, December 10, 1999) which included a description of the Church's traditional form it entitled, "This is the Church of God in Christ: Its Pattern of Organization" (Nesbitt, 1965, p. 23). This document addressed the organizational structure of the Church, the appointive powers of the Senior Bishop, the immutable pattern of the Church, and the confusion, which would result from changing the Church. The document clearly states the position of Bishop O. T. Jones, Sr., and his supporters:

THIS IS THE CHURCH OF GOD IN CHRIST
Its Pattern of Organization
Therefore, since we have received this wonderful ministry, having obtained mercy, we take this method of setting forth what we understand to be a God-accepted rule to govern the church. We hold the holy scriptures as contained in the Old and New Testaments as our rule of faith and practice …

-from the Preface of the
OFFICIAL MANUAL,
CHURCH OF GOD IN CHRIST
(Note: this passage does not appear in the
preface to the current [1973] Official Manual)

The "Pattern" - Same for National, State, Local

1. The same scriptural "pattern" that is followed by the National Church for its order and government is likewise followed by the State and Local works for their order and government

Hence, each office, department, and meeting that exists on the National level may likewise exist - in its counterpart - on the State and Local levels. In other words; the Church is organized on the State and Local levels just like it is organized on the National level.

In the *National Church* there is a General Assembly, presided over by the *Senior Bishop*.

In the *State* there is a *State Assembly*, presided over by the *State Bishop*.

In the *Local Church* there is a *Local Assembly*, presided over by the *Pastor*.

2. This is because the Church of God in Christ, as an organized body of believers, *began* as a National body.

This is indicated in our Church's history.

Later in the same year 1907, Elder C. H. Mason called a meeting in Memphis, Tenn., of all the ministers who believed in receiving the baptism of the Holy Ghost according to the scriptures Acts 2:4 ...

These brethren formed the first General Assembly of the Church of God in Christ, whose faith was founded upon the doctrine of the Apostles as received on the day of Pentecost.

> • OFFICIAL MANUAL,
> CHURCH OF GOD IN CHRIST,
> 1957 Ed., p. 8-9

3. Thus, the Church of God in Christ on the State and Local levels looks to the Church on the National level for clarification of the "pattern" it is to follow in its faith and order and government.

"The General Assembly is the only doctrine expressing and law-making authority of the Church."

> • Church Constitution, Art. 7; par. 1

4. The "pattern" of the Church's organization is not a mere human arrangement; its ministries and offices are of Divine origin. Hence we read -

> "And God hath set some in the Church, first apostles, secondarily prophets, thirdly teachers ..." — I Cor. 12:28

> "And he gave some, apostles; and some, prophets; and some evangelists; and some pastors and teachers ..." —Eph. 4:11

> "All members have not the same office." — Rom. 12:4

5. Our Church believes that the office of Senior Bishop, which is the office of the Chief Apostle, was placed in the Church by the Lord - just as was the office of State Bishop or State Overseer and Pastor were placed in our Church by the Lord. This is indicated in our Church's official history.

> "The Lord gave Elder C. H. Mason to be Chief Apostle, to which the whole assembly accepted." - from "History" in OFFICIAL MANUAL CHURCH OF GOD IN CHRIST, 1957 Ed. P. 9

The Appointive Powers of the Office of Senior Bishop

1. In the Church of God in Christ, the Senior Bishop appoints State Overseers or State Bishops and Heads of National Departments. This is according to our Constitution.

> "The Overseer will be appointed by the Senior Bishop and may be removed for Cause by the Senior Bishop or his appointee."

> • Church Constitution, Art. 11, par. 1

"Said National Officers [of National Departments] to be appointed by Senior Bishop."
- Church Constitution, Art. 13, par. 19

2. The appointive powers of the office of the Senior Bishop are in accord with the scriptural "pattern" which gives the Leader on each level of the church (national, state, and local) the power of appointment.

"For this cause left I thee in Crete, that thou shouldest [sic] set in order the things that are wanting, and ordain elders in every city, as I had appointed thee." - Titus 1:5

This scripture which gives to one man (the Sate Bishop) authority to appoint pastors in the state also gives one man (the Senior Bishop) the authority to appoint Bishops over the states.

Note: The Scripture does not read: for this cause left **WE** thee in Crete. Rather it reads: for this cause left **I** thee in Crete.

3. The appointive powers of the office of Senior Bishop on the national level follow, fundamentally the same 'pattern' as is followed by the Leaders of the Church on every level of its existence (national, state, and local). Hence:

On the national level the Senior Bishop appoints Heads of National Departments and the Bishops (Overseers) of States.

On the state level, the State Bishop appoints State Officials and the Pastors to local churches in the state.

On the local level, the Pastor appoints Local Officials and Heads of Local Auxiliaries.

4. The Church of God in Christ has been greatly blessed of the Lord by following its God-given "pattern." Our official history says:

> "Under his leadership [that is the leadership of the first Senior Bishop] the Church has witnessed a great triumph and growth."

- "History" in the OFFICIAL MANUAL, CHURCH OF GOD IN CHRIST, 1957

Our Church Has Covenanted Not to Change Its Spiritual "Pattern"

1. While it is true, that the General Assembly has the authority to make laws for the Church, it is *not* true that the General Assembly has the authority to change the "pattern" of the Church's leadership. Article 9 in our Church Constitution restricts the powers of the General Assembly in this regard.

> " (a) It [the General Assembly] shall not set aside or change any of our articles of faith, nor shall it establish any new doctrines contrary to the doctrines that now exist in the church.
>
> (b) The General Assembly shall not abolish our representative form of government *nor the General Superintendency* [sic], *nor deprive it of any of the authority given it by this Constitution.*"

If the Church is to be consistent with its history, organizational structure and composition, and Constitution, the General Superintendency [sic] not only consists of State Bishops (who presently compose the Board of Bishops); but also the office of Senior Bishop.

For it was by authority of the Board of Bishops, that the office of Senior Bishop was filled after the death of the late first Senior Bishop. The present Senior Bishop was elected to this office by the General Assembly in 1962, which was an election held by the authority of the Board of Bishops.

2. Hence, the General Assembly cannot be legally convened by any person or group for the purpose of depriving either State Bishops (or State Overseers) or the Senior Bishop of any of their constitutional appointive powers.

   Overseers are granted by our Constitution the power to appoint and assign Pastors, District Superintendents, and to preside over their respective State Assemblies.
   • Church Constitution, Article 11

   The Senior Bishop is granted by our Constitution the power to appoint State Overseers and the Heads of National Departments.
   • Church Constitution, Articles 11, 13

3. The General Assembly has been given the authority, by our Constitution, to make Amendments to our Constitution. However, the General Assembly has been prohibited from Amending Article 9 of our Constitution, which among other things, prohibits the General Assembly from depriving the Church General Superintendency [sic] (which includes both State Bishops and Senior Bishops) from exercising the appointive powers vested in their respective offices.

4. These constitutional restrictions upon the General Assembly are an additional safeguard built-in the Constitution to protect the "pattern" of the Church

against any possible subversion, even by the General Assembly.

Contemplate the Confusion if Our God-given "Pattern" Were Subverted

1. In the Scriptures, the Church is found in all its spiritual and structural wholeness wherever any fellowship of believers are found. The only difference in the Church anywhere on any level is size.

   Whatever "gifts," or "administrations," or "operations," or "offices" God is said to have placed in the Church, these should be operative in every Church - large or small, national or local, then and now.

2. Hence, if "twelve" men or a "board" *ought* to lead the Church on the national level, then "twelve" men or a "board" *ought* to lead the Church on the state and local levels. For the scriptures recognized no different "pattern" for the national or larger than for the state or smaller body.

   This would mean that, instead of one man, there ought to be
   > "twelve" Co-Chairmen of each national, state and local board
   > "twelve" Co-General Secretaries and "twelve" State Secretaries
   > "twelve" Co-State Bishops of each state
   > "twelve" Co-Pastors of each local church.

3. Obviously, if our church or any organization were to follow this latter "pattern" in its leadership, it would inevitably fall into confusion and disintegration. And

   "God is not the author of confusion, but of peace, as in all churches of the saints" I Cor. 14:33

4. Throughout the Scriptures and church history, God has always made choice of one man to be the chief leader for His people at any one time and place. In our church - he is our Senior Bishop.

5. This chief leader has always been given by the Lord authority not given to any other office or person or group of persons.

6. Do not the holy scriptures, especially in Numbers 16, warn and denounce any policy or procedure - undertaken by any person or group, deliberately or unintentionally - which seeks to subvert or overthrow the Divinely chosen leader?
   "For rebellion is as the sin of witchcraft." I Sam 15:23 (Nesbitt, 1965, p. 23)

The foregoing statement concerning COGIC's Pattern of Organization makes several statements (set forth in separate sections) that are supported by the facts and it makes several statements that it does not adequately support.

Under the first section, which deals with "The Pattern" this document presents a credible case. As in the case with each successive section, the case is presented under a series of numbered points.

Point 1 uses logic and well-known fact to establish that the pattern existing at the time of the power struggle was the accepted pattern on the national, the state and, the local level.

Point 2 appeals to a quote from the 1957 edition (p. 8-9) of the *Official Manual* of the Church of God in Christ to establish that COGIC began as a national body [the apparent lack of legal incorporation as previously outlined in this work not withstanding]. The quote is accurate, appropriately cited, and it does reveal that the Church was founded as a national body. This quote is also in subsequent editions of the *Official Manual* including the current (1973) edition.

Point 3 seeks to establish the fact that the national church legally provides the pattern for the state and local church. To do this the document appropriately uses an accurate quote from the *Official Manual* (Art. 7: par. 1, 1957). This quote is also in subsequent editions of the *Official Manual* including the current (1973) edition.

Point 4 attempts to trace COGIC's organizational pattern to three (accurately quoted) scriptural passages of God's gift of offices to the Church. These scriptural references are open to interpretation and do not provide a clear theological support for the position advanced.

Point 5 states that "the office of Senior Bishop, which is the office of the Chief Apostle, was placed in the Church by the Lord" (Nesbitt, 1965, p. 23). To support this position the document accurately quotes the 1957 edition of the *Official Manual*. This quote does establish that fact that Elder C. H. Mason was accepted as a divinely appointed Chief Apostle by COGIC's founding assembly as represented in the 1957 *Official Manual*. This quote is not found in the current (1973) edition of the *Official Manual*.

The second section examines the appointive powers of the office of the Senior Bishop.

Point 1 appropriately uses two accurate quotes from the 1957 edition of the *Official Manual* that do outline the appointive powers of the Senior Bishop.

Point 2 attempts to use one (accurately quoted) scriptural reference (Titus 1:5) to establish the pattern of church appointments. Again, these scriptural references are open to interpretation and do not provide a clear theological support for the position advanced.

Point 3 uses commonly accepted practice, which both the 1957 and the 1973 editions of the *Official Manual* support, to establish that the appointive powers of the office of the Senior Bishop follows the same pattern as the appointive powers of other offices on the state and local levels. This point does not quote the appropriate sections of the (then current) Church Constitution, which would have supported this assertion.

Point 4 refers to COGIC's history as set forth in the 1957 (and echoed in the 1973) *Official Manual.* This reference points out that under the administration of the first Senior Bishop the Church experienced tremendous growth. This fact is then extrapolated to mean that it was the pattern, and not the person, that fostered this growth.

The third section intimates that COGIC does not have the power to change its own organizational pattern.

Point 1 actually addresses three separate issues. First, it looks at the issue stated in the heading to the section; it does this by quoting COGIC's constitution as set forth in the 1957 *Official Manual.* This accurately quoted passage clearly states that the General Assembly does not have the power to change the articles of faith, promulgate new doctrines contrary to the established doctrines, nor to deprive the General Superintendency of the authority given to it by the constitution. This clearly stated restriction on the authority of the General Assembly is not present in constitution as presented in the 1973 *Official Manual.* Secondly, this section states that to be consistent with the church's history, organizational structure, composition, and Constitution the General Superintendency includes Senior Bishops as well as State Bishops. The document does not offer any proof to support this contention. The third issue addressed by this point is that it was by the authority of the Board of Bishops that the election of Bishop O. T. Jones, Sr. as Senior Bishop took place. This assertion is not supported by any objective, external proof.

Point 2 starts with the word "Hence" (Nesbitt, 1965, p. 23), which *The Oxford Dictionary and Thesaurus:*

American Edition says means "for this reason or as a result of inference" (Abate, 1996, p. 684). In a document attempting to prove a position through a logical set of facts and statements this seems to be a poor choice of words, inasmuch as point 2 deals with who has the power to convene meetings of the General Assembly for the purpose of depriving officials of their appointive powers and not the ideas advanced in point 1. As proof for the assertion made, point 2 accurately quotes two passages from COGIC's constitution as presented in the 1957 *Official Manual.* The passage that deals with the appointive powers of State Bishops is echoed in the constitution as presented in the 1973 *Official Manual* while the one addressing the appointive powers of the Senior Bishop is not. Neither of these passages speaks to the question of who is empowered to convene the General Assembly.

Point 3 returns to the direct objective of this section by stating (without quoting) that Article 18 (Amendments) of COGIC's constitution as presented in the 1957 *Official Manual* does in fact prohibit the General Assembly from amending sections a, b, or c, (which speaks of the authority of the General Superintendency) of Article 9. This restriction is not found in COGIC's constitution as set forth in the 1973 *Official Manual.*

Point 4 sums up this section without adding any additional proof to substantiate its claims.

The fourth and final section of this Pattern of Organization document asks the reader to "Contemplate" the "Confusion" it says will be the result of changing ("Subverting") what it calls, "Our God-given Pattern" (for all quotes in this paragraph Nesbitt, 1965, p. 23).

Point 1 makes an argument that the Church should be the same everywhere, "large or small, national or local, then and now" (Nesbitt, 1965, p. 23), there is no specific proof offered to support this assertion.

Point 2 builds upon the idea expressed in point 1 stating that if "'Twelve' men or a 'board'" (Nesbitt, 1965, p. 23), as opposed to one man (a Senior Bishop) ought to lead the church then there should be 12 people in every position. No proof beyond the logic expressed in point 1 is advanced in support of this argument.

Point 3 merely contends that if any organization followed the 12-man pattern spoken of in Point 2 would "Obviously" (Nesbitt, 1965, p. 23) fall into confusion. It then goes on to cite the scriptural passage I Corinthians 14:33 that states that God is not the author of confusion. This scriptural reference is not germane to the idea presented in this point.

Point 4 states that "Throughout the Scriptures and church history" (Nesbitt, 1965, p. 23) God has consistently chosen a one-man type of leadership and in COGIC it is the Senior Bishop. This argument is unsupported and contravenes the well-known evidence from the Acts of the Apostles and the Pre-Nicene Fathers that although the Apostles and early bishops acted autonomously, they also convened councils for guidance and clarification of doctrine.

Point 5 is merely a statement that seems as if it should have been the final sentence of point 4.

Point 6 makes reference to Numbers 16, which relates the rebellion of Korah against Moses and Aaron in the wilderness and then generalizes this passage to "any policy or procedure - undertaken by any person or group, deliberately or unintentionally - which seeks to subvert or overthrow the Divinely chosen leader" (Nesbitt, 1965, p. 23). This statement leaves one with the unstated rhetorical question, "Who is this divinely chosen leader that is herein referred to?" I believe the implied answer is that Senior Bishop O. T. Jones, Sr. is this divinely appointed leader. This point ends with the quote from I Samuel 15:23 "For rebellion is as the sin of witchcraft" (Nesbitt, 1965, p. 25) thus implicitly charging the opponents of Bishop Jones with the heinous crime of witchcraft.

When the social scientist Max Weber first described bureaucracies, he did not mean the synonym for a person-nel-bloated, red-tape strangled, inefficient, writing and recording organization that the word conjures up in current usage. He meant instead an organization that operated with the impersonal precision of a machine and was the epitome of the mechanistic metaphor advanced by Gareth Morgan in his seminal book *Images of Organization,* In his initial description of bureaucratic organizations:

> Weber's analysis was based on the assumption that the members of an organization will in fact com-ply with the rules and obey orders. He asked on what basis do the rule-promulgators and order-givers obtain their legitimate authority. He paid no attention to the problem of establishing the legitimacy of authority in the face of opposition and a refusal to consent on the part of the governed. This is a situa-tion frequently met, for example, when a bureau-cratic authority attempts to supplant a traditionalistic one, or when the rule of the expert or rational-legal wielder of power is faced with resistance. (Pugh & Hickson, 1993, p. 7)

This situation was clearly "a struggle for power" (Dubois, 1966; Synan, 1986, p. 55; Thomas, 1966, p. 1) cast in the language of a bureaucratic organization. Both sides claimed to base their actions upon the rules and regulations as they then existed in the Church. For authority and organi-zational legality they appealed to the organizational position occupied by the persons initiating the actions.

There was another document that was circulated within The Church of God in Christ through *THE COGIC VOICE.*

This document, "TO MAKE IT PLAIN" (Nesbitt, 1965, p. 26) discuses the allegations made by the General Secretary and the Executive Board of the Church of God in Christ against Senior Bishop O. T. Jones, SR and provides a response to each:

TO "MAKE IT PLAIN"

... Write the vision, and make it plain upon tables, that he may run that readith [sic] it. For the vision is yet for an appointed time, but at the end it shall speak, and not lie; though it tarry, wait for it; because it will surely come, it will not tarry. Behold, his soul which is lifted up is not upright in him: but the Just shall live by faith. (Habakkuk 2:2-4)

Reasonable men may disagree, but reasonable, intelligent, honest, saved, "Holy Ghost-Filled" men will hear the truth about any matter and admit the same. It is not very difficult to read certain statements and arrive at certain conclusions. The answer we get, in many instances, is determined by our attitude at the time when we are reading, our desires, our intentions, our intellectual abilities, our exposure, and our direction.

Sometimes men who are really interested in the Truth - and will stand for it - like to find out just how many people will stand with them. They send out certain statements to watch the response of the readers. In such a case, the writer may not be voicing what he knows to be the Truth, or even what he believes himself.

Because it is assumed that all true members of the Church of God in Christ take the happening of the Church very seriously, and because certain recent documents, inconsistent with the Spirit of the Church, have been circulated throughout the Church; this space is devoted to a critical analysis of that certain document, dated February 8, 1965, under the heading of "Executive Board Church of God in Christ, Inc." and written over the signatures of the General Secretary and other "Executives" acting with him. In this space we are seeking the **TRUTH** of the **MATTERS** set forth.

We will seek to analyze the document by setting forth **THE ALLEGATION** BY THE "Executive Board," and then follow it with **THE FACTUAL** picture or analysis of the matter involved.

THE ALLEGATION: - that "under the constitution and by-laws of the Church of God in Christ, there is no provision whatsoever for a "Senior Bishop," after the death of the late revered Bishop C. H. Mason;"

THE FACT IS - There is no place in the COGIC Constitution which terminates the Office of Senior Bishop with the death of the late Bishop C. H. Mason.

THE constitution anticipates and provides for the continuation of the Office of Senior Bishop in that it expressly sets forth:

"the Overseer will be appointed by the Senior Bishop and may be removed for cause by the Senior Bishop or his appointee." COGIC Const. [sic] Art. 11; par. 1

"Said national officers (of National Departments) to be appointed by Senior Bishop" COGIC Const. [sic] Art. 13; par. 10

THERE is nothing in the constitution which establishes any other appointive authority for these vital offices and positions in the Church. It seems reasonable to conclude that it was intended that the incumbent in the Office of Senior Bishop would make the appointments, no matter what his name might be.

NOTE: When the late Bishop C. H. Mason died the "pattern" which God had given for the Church did not die with him. It should also be remembered that God did not die either. **THANK GOD! HE LIVES.**

THE ALLEGATION: - that "the constitution and by-laws expressly state that on the death of Bishop Mason, the power, authority and government of the Church shall vest in the Executive Board."

THE FACT IS - The COGIC Constitution provides: " ... Bishop C. H. Mason, the present Senior Bishop, shall retain his present power and authority during his life-time, but upon his death said authority shall revert to the Board of Bishops." COGIC Const. [sic] Art. 7; par 2

THE constitution does not mention "Executive Board," for there was no such creature at that time. And by the constitution there is no such creature at this time.

THE ALLEGATION: - That "this board was created by the late Bishop C. H. Mason."

THE FACT IS - There is no record which shows when or that the late Bishop C. H. Bishop Mason, serving in the Office of Senior Bishop during his life on earth, created the "Executive Board."

THE ALLEGATION: - that "its power and authority was recognized and ratified by the General Assembly ... on several occasions."

THE FACT IS - There is no record to establish that "its power and authority was recognized and ratified by the General Assembly ... on several occasions."

> **NOTE:** Even if the allegations of the "Executive Board" were true, they allege that the "General Assembly" attempted to do what the COGIC Constitution Art. 9 (b) expressly forbids it to do.

> **THE GENERAL ASSEMBLY** "shall not abolish ... the General Superintendency [sic]." To seek to place the "Executive Board" in a position above the Office of Senior Bishop is to oppose one of the Cardinal Principles of our Church.

THE ALLEGATION: - THAT "Bishop O. T. Jones has, since 1962, usurped the power of the Executive Board, and allogated [sic] unto himself the authority to appoint Bishops, Overseers and other Officials of the Church."

THE FACT IS - With the authority and approval of the Board of Bishops of the Church, into whose hands the power of the Church was vested upon the death of the late Bishop C. H. Mason, COGIC Const. [sic] Art. 7, par. 2, Bishop O. T. Jones was duly elected Senior Bishop of the Church of God in Christ by the General Assembly, 55th Annual Convocation, Memphis, Tennessee, December 7, 1962. This is in the RECORD and the fact of the same was officially released to the world by our National Public Relations Office.

THE "Executive Board" is not a constitutional board of the Church. There is nothing to show any rights, authority or power which the "Executive Board" was possessed of; therefore, the question of usurpation of their authority is an unreasonable claim.

NOTE: Judging from the attempted actions of the "Executive Board" in the document under analysis, it appears that the said Board might be guilty of the act of which it wrongfully accuses our beloved and duly elected Senior Bishop O. T. Jones.

SENIOR Bishop O. T. Jones has not "abrogated unto himself the authority to appoint Bishops, Overseers and other Officials of the Church." To the contrary, he did make appointments within the authority granted the Office of Senior Bishop by the COGIC Constitution, Art. 11; par 1 and Art. 13; par. 10

NOTE: The term "abrogated" means "to annul by the authority or by later enactment; abolish, cancel or repeal." The term is improperly used and is inconsistent with the allegations of the "Executive Board." In this very statement they admit that the accusations made against the Senior Bishop are false.

There is a word arrogate (to take, demand, or claim unreasonably or presumptuously; assume; usury) which could have been used by the "Executive Board," but even if they had used the word arrogate, the Senior Bishop would not be guilty of their allegations because he assumed or usurped nothing. The COGIC Constitution gave him all the authority which he used and is now using.

THE ALLEGATION: - that the Senior Bishop's Appointments of Bishops, Overseers and other National Officers "were unlawful and without authority."

THE FACT IS - The Senior Bishop's appointments were legal and within the appointive authority granted to the Office of Senior Bishop, Art. 11, par. 1, and Art. 13; par. 10

THE ALLEGATION: - that the "Executive Board" was making the appointment of six state Bishops and two National Officers who had previously been appointed by the Senior Bishop.

THE FACT IS - The "Executive Board" has no appointive authority in the Church. The fact is, there is nothing to show that it has any authority in the Church. Such an action is unreasonable, inconsistent with principles of mutual respect, and is not worthy to be followed. Only the Senior Bishop of the Church has appointive authority in the categories under discussion here.

THE ALLEGATION: - that the Senior Bishop was being officially notified "to cease and desist from making any appointments."

THE FACT IS - A board which has no constitutional or other status in the Church has no authority to notify the duly elected Senior Bishop of the Church what he must do. This is in poor taste, it is not "good manners" and it is a nullity.

NOTE: As duly elected Senior Bishop and Chairman of the General Assembly; it is the Senior Bishop's responsibility to defend the Church against its enemies, within or without. The Senior Bishop not only has power to appoint, but he also has the authority to remove from office those who give cause for such removal. It should be remembered that, in this Church boards do not tell the Senior Bishop what he is to do. And in the states the boards do not tell the Bishop what he must do.

THE ALLEGATION: - that "from and after this time, the Executive Board will **NOT** recognize appointments made by the "Senior Bishop," and we also serve notice that he nor any appointee he may name will act at their own risk and peril."

THE FACT IS - This statement is an admission by the "Executive Board' that it has no authority, and that it has no position to take any action relative to appointments made by the Senior Bishop or to any of his appointees. The Lord must have led them to conclude "he nor any appointee he may name will act at their own risk and peril."

NOTE: It is interesting to note that the Supreme Court of the State of Texas in the Case: Church of God in Christ No. 1, Silsbee, Texas VS R. J. Darrett, seems to suggest that the "Executive Board" has no legal standing in the Church of God in Christ. If the "Executive Board" has no legal standing in the Church, doesn't it raise a question among reasonable men as to whether or not that board is acting "at their own risk and peril?" (Nesbitt, 1965, p. 26-28)

This document, "TO MAKE IT PLAIN," besides expressing the position and tone of Bishop Jones' supporters, catalogs the specific accusations leveled against Jones by the Executive Board. What follows is an item by item analysis of the foregoing document beginning with the introduction.

The opening paragraph of the introduction explicitly states that all

"reasonable, intelligent, honest, saved, Holy Ghost-Filled men will hear the *truth* (emphasis added) about any matter and admit the same" (Nesbitt, 1965, p. 26). This implicitly says that anyone who disagrees with this truth must not be reasonable, intelligent, honest, etc.

The second paragraph opens a door for the leader who has leveled the "Allegations" (Nesbitt, 1965, p. 26-28) to rejoin the fold, to recant by saying he merely sent out the Allegations "to watch the response of the readers" (Nesbitt, 1965, p. 26) and that he wasn't truly "voicing what he knows to be the Truth, or even what he believes himself" (Nesbitt, 1965, p. 26).

The last two paragraphs of the introduction make it clear that the Allegation, in the estimation of the author, is spurious and needs to be followed and clarified by what the author of this document says he is searching for, "the TRUTH of the MATTER" (Nesbitt, 1965, p. 26), which he labels, "THE FACT IS" (Nesbitt, 1965, p. 26-28)

The first Allegation is that there is no provision in the COGIC Constitution for the continuation of the Office of Senior Bishop after the death of Bishop C. H. Mason. The rebuttal, which follows this first allegation, uses deductive logic to reach several conclusions. First, it states that since COGIC's Constitution does not call for the termination of the Office of Senior Bishop after the death of C. H. Mason it must inherently continue. It then goes on to cite two separate articles of the 1952 constitution which state that there are certain functions (appointments) that the Senior Bishop is called upon to carry out. The author then deduces that since these functions are necessary and no one else is named by the constitution as competent to carry them out except the Senior Bishop the Office of Senior Bishop must therefore continue. This first set of "The Allegation and The Fact Is" ends by explicitly saying that the "pattern" of organization for COGIC was given to Bishop Mason by God. It implicitly says that since God did not die when Bishop Mason did this pattern should go on as well.

The second section correctly points out that the Allegation which here states "that on the death of Bishop Mason, the power, authority, and government of the Church shall be vested in the Executive Board" (Nesbitt, 1965, p. 26) is erroneous. According to the 1952 COGIC Constitution, which was in force at the time of Bishop Mason's death, these powers "shall revert to the Board of Bishops" (Pleas, 1991, p. 87). This section also points out correctly that according to the constitution then current in COGIC, the Executive Board is never mentioned.

The third Allegation is that the Executive Board was created by Bishop Mason. This is answered in the corresponding The Fact Is with the unsupported statement that the Allegation is false.

The fourth Allegation states that the Executive Board's "power and authority was recognized and ratified by the General Assembly" (Nesbitt, 1965, p. 27). The Fact Is section answers this allegation in two ways. First it states that there is "no record to establish" (Nesbitt, 1965, p. 27) such a recognition of the Executive Committees power by the General Assembly. Secondly, this allegation continues with an appeal to the then current COGIC Constitution. This appeal is not to a statement in the constitution that directly supports this position but instead to an oblique reference in Article 9 (b) which refers to a restriction of the powers of the General Assembly. This section reads in full "The General Assembly shall not abolish our representative form of government nor the General Superintendency [sic], nor deprive it of any of the authority given it by this Constitution" (Pleas, 1991, p. 88). This rebuttal section quotes this section in an abbreviated form when it says, "The General

Assembly shall not abolish ... the General Superintendency [sic]" (Nesbitt, 1965, p. 27). Although abbreviated this section does carry the sense of the constitutional article (at least as far as its relevance to the so-called General Superintendency [sic]). The final statement of this section is expressed as the logical conclusion to the foregoing argument, "To seek to place the 'Executive Board' in a position above the Office of Senior Bishop is to oppose one of the Cardinal Principles of our church" (Nesbitt, 1965, p. 27).

The fifth Allegation contends that Bishop O. T. Jones has usurped the power to appoint Bishops and other officials. This is rebutted by the corresponding Fact Is section that points out that according to the then current constitution (Art. 7; par. 2) when Bishop Mason died all of his power was vested in the Board of Bishops and that with their authority and approval Bishop Jones was elected Senior Bishop by the General Assembly at the 55th Holy Convocation on December 7, 1962. This section also makes an attack upon the Executive Board. It states that the Executive Board is not a constitutionally established board of the church and that as such any power or authority it was attempting to exert or enforce was in itself a usurpation of legitimate power. Returning to its defense of Bishop Jones and his actions this section again accurately cites articles of the then current constitution (Art. 11; par. 1 and Art. 13; par. 10) to prove that the Office of Senior Bishop is vested with appointive powers.

The sixth Allegation repeats the charge that Bishop Jones' appointments "were unlawful and without authority" (Nesbitt, 1965, p. 27). The Fact Is section cites the same articles used in the preceding section to refute the charge.

The seventh Allegation states that the Executive Board was making appointments to supercede the previous appointments made by Senior Bishop O. T. Jones, Sr. The Fact Is sections makes the unsupported rebuttal that the

Executive Board has no appointive power and that the senior Bishop does.

The eighth Allegation officially notifies Senior Bishop O. T. Jones, Sr. "to cease and desist from making any appointments" (Nesbitt, 1965, p. 28). The Fact Is section once again points out that (in its opinion) the Executive Board was acting without any legitimate authority. It also points out that this type of actions were in "poor taste" not "good manners" and "a nullity" (Nesbitt, 1965, p. 28). None of these arguments are supported by any objective evidence.

The ninth, and final, Allegation is a threat that states the Executive Board will not recognize any appointments made by Senior Bishop Jones and that Jones and his appointees "will act at their own risk and peril" (Nesbitt, 1965, p. 28). Not surprisingly the accompanying Fact Is section also ends with the counter-threat that the Executive Board was acting "at their own risk and peril" (Nesbitt, 1965, p. 28). For support the Fact Is section cites a Texas Court case, Church of God in Christ, No. 1, Silisbee, Texas VS R. J. Darrett, which it contends suggests that the Executive Board "has no legal standing in the Church" (Nesbitt, 1965, p. 28). In the court case referenced there is no mention of the Executive Board and no direct reference to the matters at hand (*Darret v. COGIC No. 1 of Silisbee, TX,*1964).

We now come to the Holy Convocation of 1965. This first Convocation after the circular letters, accusations and counter charges set the stage for all that was to follow and is therefore dealt with here in an extensive manner. The confusion of the Church is aptly portrayed in a quote from Missionary Lucille J. Cornelius (a contemporaneous observer and Historical Recording Secretary of the denomination) in her book *The Pioneer* (1975) when she says:

> We were invited by Bishop D. Lawrence Williams to the 58th Holy Convocation and to honor

Bishop O. T. Jones on Official Day [An Official Day is a day set aside to honor a specific official. On that day this official will present the message and receive a personal collection from the attendees]. We were invited by the Executive Board to the same Convocation to honor Founder's Day as a commemoration of Bishop C. H. Mason and that would be the action of the day and not an official day for Bishop Jones. (p. 81)

The confusion continued throughout this first divided Convocation. The Executive Committee, which prepared and published the schedule of the meeting, changed the format from its traditional 20 days to one week. Historically, the Holy Convocation had always begun with 72 hours of fasting and prayer led by the Senior Bishop. This first three days of fasting was very important for symbolic reasons. It was seen as a "gesture away from the living space being left behind and the ritual act indicating that the Saints had arrived at their destination" (Clemmons, 1996, p. 77). Now the fasting still occurred and mornings consisted of prayer, but preaching and organizational business consumed the afternoons and nights.

Nothing points out the confusion, contradiction, and turmoil more than the proceedings of the first day of this first divided Convocation. The reigning Senior Bishop had presided in every other year except 1962 when there was no Senior Bishop, but this year (1965) "the Executive Board took over and Bishop A. B. McEwen and Bishop J. S. Bailey presided" (Cornelius, 1975, p, 81). When this fractious Convocation opened, it was Bishop O. M. Kelly who introduced the day's speaker, Bishop S. Crouch. As the Convocation began, Senior Bishop O. T. Jones, Sr. was on the platform but he was not in charge of the day's events. At the end of the days services Bishop Jones got up:

To lead us in prayer he asked all to lay hands on each other and urged all to go through the fast for three days and nights. "Let us finish our consecration before we raise any money, let us get wholehearted with God. What we need is God. Our trouble now is mostly over money, we don't want to mix it up, let the money go, and let God." He began to sing the song, "God Can Do Anything But Fail," then he led us in prayer. (Cornelius, 1975, p. 82)

Immediately after Bishop Jones was finished Bishop A. B. McEwen,

Chairman of the Executive Board, stood up and said, "We have heard from heaven today, we certainly did enjoy Bishop Crouch" (Cornelius, 1975, p. 82) thus ignoring completely the remarks of the Senior Bishop. And then as if to reinforce his challenge to traditional procedure, Bishop McEwen went on to directly contradict the Senior Bishop by saying "an offering was necessary and that they must take an offering" (Cornelius, 1975, p. 82). Then an offering was taken showing who was actually in charge of the proceedings.

Missionary Cornelius, as an eyewitness to the occurrences of this Convocation, recorded her impressions in vivid language and minute detail. During the second day's service she reflected:

The Chairman of the Executive Board presided and Bishop O. T. Jones was not allowed to talk any more on this day. The battle for authority was on. It had begun with the say as to whether or not there would be an offering taken during the fast. The Executive Board had won, and the offering was taken. (Cornelius, 1975, p. 82)

On the next night, Bishop M. C. Williams was the Master of Ceremonies. Bishop Jones' main supporter, Bishop Ranger, read the scripture and Bishop Jones was honored as Senior Bishop and given time to say a few words. He was immediately followed by Bishop McEwen, who was also given time to say a few words. Bishop Jones or his supporters were not heard from again until Sunday, November 14.

As stated earlier, Bishop Jones and his supporters had sent out invitations to this Convocation stating that the Sunday service would be Official Day while the Executive Board had said that it would be Founders Day. Missionary Cornelius records the beginning of the day in these words, "Our late Bishop Mason [sic] pictures were hung up and waved as banners over the podium. This day marked another part of the battle for authority ... we could plainly see it was Founder's Day and things moved smoothly all day" (Cornelius, 1975, p. 83).

After the morning speaker, Bishop Bailey presented Bishop Jones as the Senior Bishop:

> As Bishop O. T. Jones stood, there was a tremendous ovation of the people as they stood crying and praising God all over the building, truly people loved this man. It was spontaneous and automatically done. It seemed they had expected him to bring the Official Message and thought he would be left out and they were so glad he was presented. Bishop Jones humbly began to thank God and sang. "God is moving by his Spirit, move O' Lord in me." He then announced he would bring his Official Message at 8 o'clock p. m. this evening. (Cornelius, 1975, p. 83)

This elicited an expression that may have been meant to clarify the situation when Mother Ann Bailey (the wife of Bishop the Vice-Chairman of the Executive Committee) stood up and said:

> I have been blessed today, we all thank God for our Senior Bishop O. T. Jones, it is not the objective of any to do away with our Senior Bishop. God wants us all together. This Church loves Bishop Jones and Bishop McEwen. We hope to carry on in Jesus name. (Cornelius, 1975, p. 83)

But Bishop McEwen made it crystal clear that the Executive Board was appealing to the rational-legal, bureaucratic framework of written guides and that they meant to be in control when he stood up and said, "We hope to carry this program as written" (Cornelius, 1975, p. 83).

The night session started according to the Executive Committee's program with the president of the Y.P.W.W., Dr. O. T. Jones, Jr., giving a talk directed at the youth. He also took the opportunity to introduce his father as the founder and former president of the Y.P.W.W. Bishop Jones' words were again followed by words by Bishop McEwen. Then Bishop L. H. Ford started speaking by saying he felt it was time for Bishop Jones and McEwen to get together for the good of the Church. He then went on to describe the depths to which this turmoil had sunk when he:

> Told of treats (<u>sic</u>) to his life and also to Bishop Washington, Bishop McEwen and others if they bothered our Senior Bishop Jones. "I went home and cried, my members ran up to me worried for my life, a policeman came up beside me and said, 'I am going to follow you wherever you go.'" (Cornelius, 1975, p. 83)

The Sunday service ended with no message by Senior Bishop Jones (instead Bishop Rimson spoke) and a collection taken by the Finance Committee for Founder's Day.

November 17 was scheduled to be Youth Day, this day was presided over by Dr. O. T. Jones, Jr., president of the Y.P.W.W. After a few short messages he presented his father, the founder of the church's youth department, Bishop Jones, who called everyone to prayer. This prayer lasted for over two hours and at the end of it just as Bishop Jones began to speak a woman came forward from the audience and said:

> I'm in the Church, you don't know me, Bishop Jones doesn't know me, but God knows me. While I was on my knees I knew God had consecrated me for something and God spoke to me to tell Bishop Jones to read Romans 8:35-38. She read the 38th verse: "For I am persuaded that neither death, nor life, nor angels, nor principalities, nor powers, nor things present, nor things to come, nor height, nor depth, nor any other creature, shall be able to separate us from the love of God, which is in Christ Jesus our Lord." Bishop Jones! Don't give up nothing God has given to you. If they take it let them take, but don't you give up nothing God has given to you. (Cornelius, 1975, p. 84)

The woman then returned to her seat and Bishop Jones said, "It is time for us to have an ear to hear what the Spirit says to the Church. We are here to bring to you the message God gave us" (Cornelius, 1975, p. 84). As the Senior Bishop hesitated for a moment the song "You Can't Make Me Doubt Him" was sung. Bishop Jones then said, "You may not be able to come back another year, rather you may not be able to come back tomorrow. God is calling us to consecration" (Cornelius, 1975, p. 84). He closed by speaking of his love for the Church and by saying that he was going to "Let his light shine" (Cornelius, 1975, p. 84). After Bishop Jones had prayed the closing prayer, Bishop Ranger stood up and asked, "Don't you think our Senior Bishop ought to have an offering?" also saying that everyone who thought so should come forward and lay an offering at the Apostle's feet (Cornelius, 1975, p. 84). Then many people lined up and came forward laying their offerings at the feet of Bishop Jones.

Then Evangelist J. T. Tucker from Los Angeles, a man known as a prophet since 1948, came forward to share a revelation, which he said God had given him at 3 A.M. that morning. The Evangelist said:

> If they didn't get together God said he would sift them like flies. If they overthrow Bishop O. T. Jones they would not live to receive it. They should carry the Convocation like Bishop Mason set it up, go back to 20 days and one Senior Bishop, no cutting short. Bishop Jones should not give up nothing if they take it they won't live to enjoy it. (Cornelius, 1075, p. 84)

After this second revelation, Bishop Jones dismissed the gathering for dinner.

The evening session on November 17, 1965 was the last session of this divided Convocation. After the first speaker the Chairman of the Executive Board, Bishop McEwen, led approximately 300 men from the Council Room into the General Assembly of the Convocation. The Chairman asked for and received time to tell the assembly what had been discussed in the executive session. After the General Secretary, Bishop J. O. Patterson read the minutes:

> After he read the minutes a controversy [sic] seemingly followed. There was a question as to who

was who in the Church. Bishop O. T. Jones, Senior Bishop had a group that believed he should preside as Bishop Mason had presided in organizing and appointing officials, also having Official Day on the only Sunday of the meeting. The Executive Board did not agree for anyone [sic] man to run the Church or usurp authority over them and the power should be in the Executive Board to execute authority in the Church. (Cornelius, 1975, p. 84)

This controversy had now come before the Convocation in an explicit form. Instead of snubs and power plays on the platform the main players and their issues now saw the light of day. How this was interpreted and how people reacted to it is expressed by the words of Missionary Lucille J. Cornelius, the Historical Recording Secretary of the denomination:

> The matter seems to be for Bishop Jones and Bishop McEwen to get together and settle who will do what. There is also a difference in opinion as to where this matter should be settled, in the General Assembly auditorium where all are present or in the Council Room with only a selected group. Bishop O. T. Jones wanted it settled in the General Assembly before all the people. Bishop A. B. McEwen wanted it settled in the Council Room so they began to disagree again. We prayed for a mutual agreement, to be made between two of the greatest men of our Church and both dearly loved. It is the feeling that if too much outside interference was not involved these two men would get together. (Cornelius, 1975, p. 84)

The Convocation had now become so openly contentious that when the 10:00 P.M. broadcast time arrived the traditional broadcast was not allowed to air (Cornelius, 1975, p. 85). Instead Bishop O. T. Jones stood up and read the scriptures Numbers 16:1-17 and 19-35. This passage deals with Korah's rebellion against Moses. This rebellion lasted until the earth opened up and swallowed the followers of the rebellion and God's fire from heaven came down and consumed the 250 leaders who were offering incense before the Lord. After reading this Bishop Jones said, "May the Lord burn the meaning of this Scripture on all our hearts" (Cornelius, 1975, p. 85). After this appeal to Scripture, several of the leading bishops tried to work out a solution right there on the platform. This effort was interrupted by a series of outbursts from the audience which were rebuked by Bishop McEwen who said, "Now if you had of listened to me all this wouldn't have been" (Cornelius, 1975, p. 85). Bishop Jones then stood up and said:

> I feel like we are all members of the Church of God in Christ. If people would come into our church tonight they would go another way. Now it is not the one who talks the loudest that is right. Let one talk for each side in order and let everybody else keep quiet. I have given my life for the promotion of the Church. Let's set a night and let the Word settle it. There is no use loosing relationship, friendship and fellowship. We must respect one another ... Now we want to do the right thing that is right that it says let's do it. It is like playing ball, when a man hits a ball and runs all around the umpire may say he's out and if the umpire says he's out, he's out because the umpire said it. Now that settles it and it is not more to it. Like it is now, we can say all we want to say and if it is not in harmony with the Constitution it is wrong. (Cornelius, 1975, p. 85)

Bishop Jones then asked Bishop McEwen for another meeting the following day to continue to work towards a settlement. The two bishops then shook hands and agreed to another meeting.

This first divided Convocation spilled outside the massive walls of Mason Temple when the *Tri-State Defender* (December 11, 1965) carried an article that touched briefly upon the controversies that raged within the International Headquarters:

> There was some discussion on the *degree of authority* (emphasis added) that should be exercised by *some boards and individuals* (emphasis added) in the church. It was agreed that the position of the executive board had previously been re-affirmed as the lawful authoritative governing power of the Church by the Elder's Council and the general assembly. The bishops pointed out, however, that "nothing could take from Bishop Jones, Jr., [sic] his honor as senior bishop." ("Church of God in Christ Approves," 1965)

Referring as it does to both the re-affirmation of the governing power of the Executive Board and the position of Bishop Jones as the Senior Bishop, this article aptly portrays the confusion that reigned at this divided convocation.

Nineteen sixty-six was fraught with contention. During this year both sides claimed to be the authoritative voice of leadership in the Church as they both attempted to lead and organize the denomination in such a way as to strengthen their own cause.

Bishop J. O. Patterson, as the General Secretary of the Executive Committee, sent out a booklet, *Official*, that attempted to explain the issues, as interpreted by the Executive Committee, to the general church population.

According to L. J. Cornelius in her book *Pioneer* in this booklet Bishop Patterson explained, "the Executive Board had tried to get Bishop O. T. Jones to meet in a Council to no avail and had taken matters in their hands to demote him and his workers" (Cornelius, 1975, p. 85).

The statement COGIC's Historical Recording Secretary was referring to said in full:

DID THE EXECUTIVE BOARD TRY TO RESOLVE THIS PROBLEM WITHOUT AN OPEN CLASH?

Yes! On many occasions the Executive Board tried to get "Bishop" Jones to meet with them. With the exception of twice to my knowledge, "Bishop" Jones refused to meet with them and those two times when he did, he would not meet without his self-appointed Advisory Board chaired by "Bishop" R. E. Ranger who had been defeated by the Elder's Council as a member of the Executive Board and who had a very hostile spirit toward the Executive Board and particularly to its Chairman, Bishop A. B. McEwen. (Patterson, 1967, p. 2)

What Bishop Patterson was referring to when he said the Executive Board "had taken matters in their hands to demote him and his workers" (Cornelius, 1975, p. 85) was a meeting held September 13, 1966 in Memphis, Tennessee wherein formal charges were lodged against Bishops Jones and Ranger. The hearing for these charges was held November 10, 1966. Although official notification was sent to both men by the Executive Committee (Patterson, 1967, p. 15-16; *Tennessee v. Jones*, 1966) neither Bishop Jones nor Bishop Ranger appeared at the hearing. The Executive Committee charged Bishop Jones with committing and Bishop Ranger with aiding and abetting Jones' commission of general activities, which the Executive Committee deemed to be:

1. Unbecoming of a Bishop of the Church of God in Christ
2. Not in the best interest of the Church of God in Christ
3. Diametrically opposed to the only appointed and authorized executive body of the National Church
4. In direct opposition to the known decisions, wishes and desires of the General Assembly of the Church of God in Christ. (Patterson, 1967, p. 15; *Tennessee v Jones*, 1966)

Specifically, the Executive Committee charged Bishops Jones and Ranger with attempting to:

1. Undermine the duly appointed and authorized executive body by appointing, without authority to do so, so-called supervisors or overseers of various states
2. Making statements and distributing literature that were apparently designed and intended to create confusion, discord, dissention and unwarranted and rebellious support within the rank and file of the Ministers and Laymen of the Church
3. Engaged in the so-called excommunication of Bishop D. A. Burton, Elder A. D. Baxter and other pastors in the state of Pennsylvania, all without justification, but only because they chose to continue to recognize the duly appointed and authorized executive body of the National Church
4. Engaged in other activities and practices all of which along with the previously mentioned acts

have been not in the best interest of the National
Church and in complete and total defiance of the
duly appointed and authorized executive body of
the Church of God in Christ. (Patterson, 1967, p.
15; *Tennessee v Jones* 1966)

According to a statement filed in the Chancery Court of
Shelby County, Tennessee over the signatures of Bishops
Bailey, Patterson, Kelly, White, Wells, Ford and McEwen:

That at the time and place, specified in the notice,
the General Council convened to hear the charges
against the defendants; that said charges were read,
and both proponents and opponents of the charges
were given an opportunity to bed [sic] heard; that the
defendant [sic] did not attend the hearing and offered
no proof in their defense; that the Council found that
the proof sustained the charges, and accordingly, by a
vote of 907 to 3, on motion properly made and seconded, it was decided as follows:

1. That the said Bishops O. T. Jones and R. E.
    Ranger be and they are [sic] hereby removed
    from their respective offices as Bishops of
    the Church of God in Christ with right to
    apply for reinstatement, after one (1) year
    from date of removal, upon repenting of their
    wrong;
2. That all acts and things done by the said O.
    T. Jones in the capacity of Chief Executive
    Officer or Senior Bishop of the Church of
    God in Christ, and all acts and things done by
    the said defendant, R. E. Ranger, in aiding
    and abetting the said O. T. Jones, are hereby
    declared null and void;

3. That notice thereof was given to the Defendant. (*Tennessee v Jones*, 1966)

For their part Bishop O. T. Jones, Sr., Bishop R. E. Ranger and their supporters ignored the actions and pronouncements of the Executive Committee and continued in their efforts to exert control of Church by making visits to various jurisdictions and continuing to appoint people to positions of leadership. Bishop Jones' reply to his trial was sent out in the now familiar form of a circular letter, which was used as a source by the press, as he tried to take his case before a wider tribunal than the Executive Board. In a front-page article in the *Tri-State Defender* (November 12, 1966) entitled "Bishop Seeks Hearing Before Entire Church" ("Bishop Seeks," 1966), Bishop Jones made his case for the actions which he and his supporters were shortly to take at the Convocation:

Bishop O. T. Jones, Sr., senior bishop of the Church of God in Christ, said in a circular sent to members of the one-million member church, that he has been charged with "conduct unbecoming a bishop of the Church of God in Christ," and told to appear before members of the Executive Board at 6 p.m. on Nov. 10 in the Elders Council Room of Mason Temple. Bishop Jones replied, "I refuse to consent to being heard or tried behind closed doors, or by persons who, in my judgement, have openly and maliciously made unsupportable and groundless attacks against my person, my ministry, my office, and my Christian character and integrity." He said that any charges of wrongdoing made against him are false, and the hearing is declared by him as senior bishop of the church to be null and void, and not binding upon anyone. "I shall answer my accusers, the Lord willing, before the entire church, called together especially for this purpose in the main auditorium of our national temple, at a time when everyone can hear and judge for himself," he said. ("Bishop Seeks," 1966)

Besides trying to set the stage for a debate directly before the delegates to the 1966 Convocation, Bishop also addressed the way in which those delegates were about to be certified. This was a crucial matter for who controlled the certification would control the Convocation. Consequently Bishop Jones used his circular letter and the newspaper interview to make his stand clear:

> The senior churchman also declared "null and void" a directive that participation and certification would be limited to "all state supervisors, and one layman delegate from each state. Every recognized bishop, elder and layman of the Church of God in Christ is eligible to participate in this General Assembly," he stated. ("Bishop Seeks," 1966)

Bishop Jones not only stated his case with regard to the charges against him, the trial the Executive Board had held, and the certification of delegates to the General Assembly he also made an offer to hear any complaints by delegates who were not certified when he finished the interview by saying, "Any bona fide members of the church should contact him, he said, if he is refused certification as a delegate" ("Bishop Seeks," 1966).

One result of this continuing attempt by both sides to control the direction of the church and its official affairs was a lawsuit brought in the 10th Judicial Circuit of Alabama. This case revolved around an action by the Executive Board (the establishing of a pro-Executive Board 2nd jurisdiction in Alabama under Bishop S. M. Bailey) and a reaction by the pro-Jones Bishop C. A. Ashworth who presided in the original Alabama jurisdiction (he removed the pastor of a church after the congregation of that church "voted to transfer affiliation to Diocese Two"). ("Senior Bishop's." 1966) The pastor refused to leave and a suit was filed in the Circuit Court protesting the action by Bishop Ashworth. The judge in the case:

> ruled in a written opinion that the "Senior Bishop" title conferred upon Bishop O. T. Jones of Philadelphia, is "purely an honorary position and his governmental powers in the national church, if any, are of an advisory nature." The jurist dismissed a suit challenging the legality of action, taken by the executive board is [sic] setting up Diocese Number 2 of the State of Alabama. ("Senior Bishop's," 1966)

Prior to the assembling of the 60th Convocation in 1966, an amazing article appeared in the *Tri-State Defender* (November 5, 1966). That the internal problems of the once solidly united denomination had become too public to be contained within the walls of the Church and too volatile to be solved through compromise seem to explode through the inflammatory rhetoric of this front-page article. Under a banner headline of "Power Fight Expected At COGIC Convocation: Church Meet Here May Be A Small Vietnam" ("Power Fight," 1966) the lead article succinctly sums up the positions of the contending sides when it states:

> Memphis will find itself with a "Vietnam" on its hands next week when delegates roll in from all parts of the world for the 60th Convocation to [sic] Church of God in Christ. This was the prediction of Dr. O. T. Jones, Jr., son of the Senior Bishop O. T.

Jones of Philadelphia, who was fired from his office as president of the Youth Department of the denomination last April by the church's executive board.

The main issue was whether Bishop Jones will be recognized as the head of the church, just as its founder, Bishop C. H. Mason was honored, or whether the church will recognize the executive board as the leading force. The main antagonists in the struggle are Bishop J. O Patterson, Sr., secretary of the executive board and a son-in-law of the late Bishop Mason, and Dr. O. T. Jones, Jr., son of the senior bishop, a title Bishop Patterson contends is only honorary. [It is interesting to note that according to this article the main antagonists are not the Senior Bishop (Jones, Sr.) and the chairman of the Executive Board (McEwen) but are instead Jones, Jr., and Patterson.] Bishop Patterson said the younger Jones was removed from office for insubordination - failing to show proper respect to the members of the executive board - and a provisional board appointed in its place. [This is the only mention of a Provisional Board.] "He was trying to usurp the authority of the executive board, did not show proper respect and believed his father should have the authority of the board," Bishop Patterson charged ... Asked if he thought the delegates would rally to the side of Bishop Jones Patterson said, "Yes, if got a house full of people like the ones who attended the convocation last year. He is in his eighties and somewhat senile at times," Bishop Patterson explained, "but he has great persuasive powers when he is at his best, and he would sway them." Since the 1965 Convocation, Bishop Jones has issued a statement on the conditions within the Church of God in Christ, and this week said that there is "a conspiracy" within the denomination. Bishop Jones said that he was recognized for two years as the senior bishop and cooperated with the church at large, and then those who had worked closely with him at his election became, "my chief opponents and adversaries." He claims he was "shamefully and publicly mistreated" by not being allowed to give his annual message, and was given nothing from Founder's Day. ("Power Fight," 1966)

When the 1966 Convocation convened, it was solidly in the hands of the Executive Committee. Through the use of rational-legal rules, regulations and bureaucratic maneuver they effectively excluded Senior Bishop O. T. Jones, Sr. and his supporters from speaking or participating in the regular proceedings until an altercation occurred at approximately 3:00 P.M. on Saturday November 12. The Executive Committee contended that:

O. T. Jones, O. T. Jones, Jr., and R. E. Ranger, got together a band of strong arm men and attempted to take over the convocation with force and violence; that it was necessary for the Bishops of the Church to call the police officials to come to the Church to restore order and to prevent injury to many delegates to the General Convocation; that they threatened to break up the convocation unless supreme authority is vested in the defendant, O. T. Jones. (*Tennessee v Jones*, 1966)

This version of the events is supported by the fact that pursuant to a Bill for Injunction and Accounting filed on November 15 in the Chancery Court of Shelby County, Tennessee by the Executive Board an injunction and an injunction bond against Bishops O. T. Jones and R. E. Ranger was issued under the signature of the Honorable Charles A. Rond. This injunction was served by Captain C. A. Hodges of the Civil Division of the Shelby County Sheriff's Department. This injunction ordered:

O. T. Jones and R. E. Ranger and all and every the persons before mentioned, and each and every of you [sic], that you and every of you [sic], do absolutely desist and refrain from interfering with the Complainants in carrying on their duties, in conducting the affairs of the Church of God in Christ, from molesting, threatening, or otherwise interfering with the complainants, or any of them, in carrying on the program of the Annual Convocation of the Church of God in Christ, in the collection of funds from delegates, in making annual or other reports, and that the defendants be enjoined from disposing of any funds or other property of said Church which is in their possession or under their control, pending further orders of this court. (*Tennessee v Jones*, 1966)

That the altercation did in fact occur is also supported by several eyewitnesses (all of whom wish to remain anonymous) who have given almost identical descriptions of the event which can be summed up in the words of one of the interviewees:

The Executive Committee was in charge on the platform and Bishops Jones and Ranger attempted to mount the platform demanding to be heard. The police were called and Bishops Jones, Ranger and their supporters were escorted out of the meeting. (Anonymous, personal conversation, December, 4, 1999)

Bishop Patterson in his *Official* (1967) chronicles this event but casts most of the onus on his followers when he states:

Yes, he believes in the Constitution, but his conspirers [sic] sought to take advantage of the Convocation and the General Church by appealing to mass psychology. In attempting to accomplish their objective, on Saturday, when the little children were in charge and participating in our National Convocation, the Jones faction of "strong arm" men staged a simulated Martin Luther King planned "march-in." This of course, backfired, the people's sympathy went to the children and those seeking to employ such methods to gain the sympathy of the people were looked upon as worldly and ungodly men. The Bible says, "a man's gift will make room for him." If God intends for you to have something, he will make room for you and place you in the hearts of the people so that they will love and respect you. (p. 20)

The vehemence and factional nature of the conflict which enveloped the 59th Convocation (1966) again boils over the public arena in a report which appeared in the *Commercial Appeal* (November 16, 1966) under the headline, "Negro Bishops Take Feud Over Leadership To Court" (Means, 1966, p. 23). The bitter and violent nature of this internecine dispute finds expression in many of the words used by the contemporaneous reporter to describe the events as they unfolded:

Chancellor Charles A. Rond will conduct a preliminary hearing at 10 a.m. today in the latest round of a *legal war* (emphasis added) involving one of the largest Negro churches in the nation. The opponents are Senior Bishop Ozro T. Jones of the Church of God in Christ, from Philadelphia, Pa., and Bishop A. B. McEwen of Memphis, chairman of the executive board of the church. The *schism* (emphasis added) *boiled over* (emphasis added) into the courts yesterday after simmering for a week at the annual convocation at Mason Temple, 938 Mason. Bishop McEwen and several other Memphians [residents of Memphis, TN.] obtained a temporary injunction from Chancellor Rond, which prohibits Bishop Jones from interfering with the collection of funds from delegates, and from disposing of any church funds or property. The request for an injunction charged that Bishop Jones and R. E. Ranger were removed from office last Thursday by the executive board for "conduct unbecoming a bishop." Bishop Jones, was elected Dec. 7, 1962, to succeed the late Senior Bishop C. H. Mason, founder of the church. Bishop Mason died in November, 1961, and *Bishop Jones' supporters* (emphasis added) claim the executive board was organized only as an interim body until the election of a new senior bishop. *Bishop McEwen's followers* (emphasis added) insist the executive board, of which Bishop Jones is the senior member, is still the governing authority of the church, and that the title of "senior bishop" is largely honorary. Bishop Jones was elected over Bishop McEwen and several other nominees. [This is the only place where a contested election for senior bishop is mentioned.] ... Bishop McEwen and Bishop J. O. Patterson, general secretary of the executive board, were listed as the principal complainants in yesterday's order, along with several other members of the board. The injunction named Dr. Ozro T. Jones, Jr. of Philadelphia, the bishop's son, and Bishop Ranger. Bishop McEwen refused to make any statement about the *rift* (emphasis added) last night. "We are the church," he said, "They are a minority group. They can say what they want." The complaint charged that several of Bishop Jones' supporters attempted "by force and violence to take over the meeting" at Mason Temple Saturday night. City police were summoned *to restore order* (emphasis added) among the *chanting and shouting* (emphasis added) delegates. ... When deputies arrived at the huge hall yesterday afternoon to serve the temporary injunction, they were accompanied by A. A. Latting, attorney for the McEwen group. Mr. Latting and another man, who Mr. Latting described as *"my witness,"* (emphasis added) were stopped at the door to the senior bishop's office by a *burly guard* (emphasis added). "You," he said, pointing at the officers, "can go in and serve your papers, but you," he pointed at Mr. Latting, "the only way you're going to get in is to *break the door down.*" (emphasis added) (Means, 1966, p. 23)

According to several eyewitnesses at least some of the delegates to this Convocation wore guns and made threats to others about what would happen to people who acted or voted wrong (Anonymous, personal communication, 1999). Both sides also attempted to use the press by giving interviews and issuing statements during the altercations and conflicts, which marked the 59th Convocation in 1966. In an interesting article in the *Memphis Press-Scimitar* (November 16, 1966) the situation was described in the following manner (as in the preceding article the agitated and warlike tone of the rhetoric used by the reporter is highlighted through the use of added emphasis):

Senior Bishop O. T. Jones today declared that the executive board of the Church of God in Christ has no authority to fire him and that he is still legally and spiritually, the head of his flock. The bishop's statement was the latest *salvo to be fired* (emphasis added) in what apparently is a *bitter interdenominational* [sic] *battle* (emphasis added) between *two factions for leadership* (emphasis added) of one of the largest Negro churches in the country. ... The *dispute* (emphasis added) is between Bishop Jones from Philadelphia, Pa., and the church's executive board, chairmaned [sic] by Bishop A. B. McEwen of Memphis. The executive board yesterday obtained a temporary injunction from Chancellor Charles Rond against Jones, Bishop R. E. Ranger of Ft. Worth and Bishop O. T. Jones. Chancellor Rond issued the injunction "restraining and enjoining" the defendants Jones, Sr. and R. E. Ranger from "interfering with the complainants from carrying out their duties ..." and from "molesting or threatening or otherwise interfering with the complainants in carrying on the program of the annual convocation." The suit alleges that Bishops Jones, Sr. and Ranger were removed from office on Nov. 10. It states that Jones, Sr. had "undertaken to usurp the executive, legislative and judicial powers of the church" after he was honored as Senior Bishop in 1962. The church's executive board charged in the bill that the three defendants last Saturday "got together a band of strong arm men and attempted to take over the convocation by force and violence," and that it was necessary to call police to *restore order* (emphasis added) ... After court, Bishop Jones and Bishop Ranger issued a joint statement for the press. They said the executive board has no constitutional authority to take over the church, that the authority is duly vested in the senior bishop. They said Bishop Jones has been refused permission to address the convocation and make his position known. They denied using "strong arm" tactics to invade Mason Temple, claiming that the policemen were put in the Temple by the other faction and intimidated their group. ("Church Controversy," 1966)

The interest of the public media in the on going struggle is evident through the continuing coverage accorded to Chancellor Rond's ruling on the original complaint filed by the Executive Board on November 16, 1966 and on the original cross-complaint filed November 17, 1966 as well as the injunctions sought by each side against the other (*Tennessee v. Jones,* 1966). This ruling was handed down on November 17, 1966 and reported in the *Commercial Appeal* (November 18, 1966) under the headline "Order Restrains Church Factions: Chancellor Rond Broadens Injunction To Include Fund Accounting" (Marks, 1966, p. 15):

Chancellor Charles Rond yesterday acted to safeguard funds of the Church of God in Christ by broadening the temporary injunction he granted last Tuesday in the fight for power by two church groups. Otherwise he left unchanged the order restraining Senior Bishop Ozro T. Jones of Philadelphia, Pa., and Bishop R. E. Ranger of Fort Worth from interfering with the church's annual convocation which ends today at Mason Temple at 938 Mason. The two bishops were barred from disposing of any funds or property now in their possession. The chancellor's ruling yesterday encompassed both the two bishops and the opposing church executive board headed by Bishop A. B. McEwen of Memphis. They were ordered to maintain accounts and records of all funds collected by them as officers of the church. Each is to give an accounting quarterly to its attorneys and the accounting presented by each faction will be turned over to the lawyers of the other group Chancellor Rond refused to consider taking any action affecting the expulsion of the two bishops from office last Thursday by the executive board. They were charged with "conduct unbecoming a bishop." He said Tennessee law gives the court no jurisdiction over any ecclesiastical matter that the church has already determined. The question is whether Bishop Jones or the executive board is the church's legally empowered body. The board holds that the title "senior bishop" conferred on Bishop Jones was only an honorary title and carried no supreme authority. The faction supporting Bishop Jones contends his election as senior bishop in 1962 by the church convocation placed leadership of the church in him. (Marks, 1966, p. 15)

On its surface this ruling sounds balanced and appears to be aimed equally at both sides (financially). But by allowing the previous injunction to stand, baring Jones from having any input at the convocation without also restraining the Executive Board it effectively handed the national church to the Executive Board by default.

Using the power of the injunction, the Executive Committee went on to complete the 1966 Convocation with such authority and credibility that the Historical Recording Secretary of the denomination L. J. Cornelius (1975) summed up her description of the event by saying, "And so you see although men may differ and some may even back-slide but the Church will never lose its power to save. 'The Gates of hell shall not prevail against it' " (p. 85).

Not surprisingly, Bishop Jones and his supporters had another version of the events which preceded and followed the serving of the Injunction of November 15. In a Cross Bill filed November 17, 1966 O. T. Jones, Sr., O. T. Jones, Jr., and R. E. Ranger charged the Executive Board as "co-conspirators" (*Tennessee v Jones*, 1966) with conspiring to:

> Usurp the lawful power, authority, and perquisites of the cross-complainant O. T. Jones and to arrogate and appropriate to themselves control over the fiscal, legislative, and doctrinal aspects of the Church of God in Christ, wholly without authority and contrary to the charter, constitution, and usages [sic] and practices of said church. In furtherance of said conspiracy, they have performed the following overt acts:

> (a) Without any authority or color of right, acting under the guise of the so-called "executive board," attempted to remove the cross-complainants from their lawful offices, well knowing that the so-called "executive board" is without power or authority so to do under the charter, constitution, or usages [sic] of church order, as had been adjudicated at the time such attempt was made.
> (b) By written and spoken words, questioning and impugning the rights, authority, and tenure of the cross-complainants.
> (c) Preventing and causing the prevention by force of the cross-complainants from having access to the floor of the convocation, and preventing the cross-complainants from answering the false charges made by the co-conspirators. (*Tennessee v Jones*, 1966)

Jones and his supporters also made various charges of fiscal improprieties on the part of the Executive Board. In answer to the specific charge of attempting to take over the convocation by force and violence the Senior Bishop's faction stated:

> Section VI of the original bill is denied in its entirety and the truth is exactly the reverse of the averments of said section of the original bill. The complainants, [the Executive Board] acting under color of the fiat to the original bill, obtained from this court, without hearing and upon the basis of false representations contained in the original bill, have refused to permit these defendants access to the floor of the national convocation, denied them the right of free speech, and denied them the right to answer to the convocation the false charges that have been made in the original bill which have now been circulated in the daily newspapers and are by force compelling these defendants [Jones & Supporters] to remain mute while the complainants are carrying on a campaign of vilification and the deliberate circulation of erroneous and untrue charges against these defendants. (*Tennessee v Jones*, 1966)

In answer to the cross-complaint an injunction was also decreed and served against the Executive Committee. There followed a series of filings, cross filings, depositions and hearings that consumed most of 1967 culminating in the Consent Decree of October 13, 1967. This Decree mandated that a Constitutional Convention should be called on January 30, 1968 to decide where the authority in the Church of God in Christ lay. This Decree also stated, "That all rights, powers and duties of the Senior Bishop and the Executive Board shall remain status quo until a final determination by the Constitutional Convention of the General Assembly" (*Tennessee v Jones*, 1966). The Decree vested power in the Church in the Board of Bishops until the Constitutional Convention. It outlined the procedures for the Convocation of 1967 and eliminated the possibility of confrontation by saying that this convocation could only deal with spiritual or ecclesiastical matters. No meeting of the Board of Bishops or the General Assembly was to be called or held prior to the Convention which would contravene either the letter or the spirit of the Decree. No appointments were to be made by either side before the Constitutional Convention. No one was to attempt change or affect the status or position of any other party to the agreement. And all delegates that were certified by their respective state assemblies would be seated (*Tennessee v Jones*, 1966).

All of these actions reflected the appeal by both sides in this power struggle to the rational-legal systems of both denominational and state bureaucracy. This gave an inherent advantage to the side that represented the vision of truly bureaucratic type of organization, the Executive Board. Bishop Jones and his adherents advocating as they did what was in essence a traditionalistic type of organization were at a fundamental disadvantage in this arena.

The relative weakness of the Jones faction was noticed by the media and commented upon in the *Commercial Appeal* (November 19, 1966) in an article entitled "Power Battling Factions See No Room For Middle Ground" (DuBois, 1966, p. 8). As in articles previously quoted, notice the use of inflammatory language in this article:

> Governing officials of the Church of God in Christ left Memphis yesterday after its 59th Holy Convocation failed to end *a power struggle* (emphasis added) that *threatens to divide* (emphasis added) the church. *The battle* (emphasis added) which has been waged quietly since the death of church founder C. H. Mason of Memphis in 1961, *erupted*

(emphasis added) into *a series of outbreaks* (emphasis added) and eventually court action this week. The only result of the 11-day meeting at Mason Temple was *a deepened entrenchment* (emphasis added) of the *rival forces* (emphasis added). The main *combatants* (emphasis added) are Senior Bishop O. T. Jones of Philadelphia, and his followers, and the executive board led by Bishops J. S. Bailey of Michigan and A. B. McEwen of Memphis. The issue is the power of the senior bishop. Bishop Jones' followers claim his power is nearly absolute. The executive board claims it has power. There is no middle ground. Bishop Mason had an iron hand, and his followers reasoned that his word was law. The bishop's failing was that he did not leave a clearly legible church constitution. The ambiguous wording of the church's charter at first led to only minor *clashes* (emphasis added) between Bishop Jones and the board. But then came the Ohio affair. The board appointed a new pastor to head the largest church in the state. Traditionally, the pastor of the church was also bishop of the state. But Bishop Jones, at almost the same time, named Robert Fields as bishop of Ohio. That one still isn't settled. Earlier this year in Alabama, the executive board went over Bishop Jones' head and split the state to form a new diocese and named A. A. Ashworth bishop. Bishop Jones voided the appointment, but Bishop Ashworth won a lawsuit and an appeal to retain his cap. This was without question the biggest setback for Bishop Jones. It gave the executive board courage to overtly challenge the senior bishop at the convocation just ended. The board accused Bishop Jones of "conduct not becoming a bishop" and won a court order to restrain the bishop's power at the convocation. Bishop Jones and his followers had *stormed* (emphasis added) from the floor of the assembly hall after police were called to quiet an *outbreak* (emphasis added) earlier this week. The bishop did not return to the convocation, and neither side has made a public invitation to work out the disagreement over a conference table. (DuBois, 1966, p. 8)

The author of this article points to the actual cause for the power struggle when he says "The bishop's failing was that he did not leave a clearly legible church constitution" (DuBois, 1966, p. 8). And he then goes on to enumerate the string of victories won by the Executive Council and ends his article with a prescient conclusion based upon the outcome of the 59th Holy Convocation and its various twists and turns. The string of victories to which this author points to include three concrete advances for their cause The first is an Alabama lawsuit that the author states was "the biggest setback for Bishop Jones" (DuBois, 1966, p. 8). A lawsuit that he said "gave the executive board enough courage to overtly challenge the senior bishop at the convocation just ended" (DuBois, 1966, p. 8). The second is the charges of "conduct unbecoming a bishop" (Dubois, 1966, p. 8) which the Executive Board successfully placed against Bishop Jones and his supporters. The third is the fact that the Executive Board "won a court order to restrain the bishop at the convocation" (DuBois, 1966, p. 8). Finally, the author astutely judges the organizational outcome of Chancellor Rond's actions when a reference is made to the executive board as being "apparently now the legal head of the church" (DuBois, 1966, p. 8).

Another contemporaneous view (which agrees in its conclusion with the preceding article) projected a picture of the 59th convocation ending with a return to harmony, unity and fellowship. Found in the *Tri-State Defender* under a headline which reads, "Power Fight Simmers As 59th Convocation Ends" (Thomas, 1966, p. 1), this article announces the election of a "president of the Church of God in Christ" (Thomas, 1966, p. 2):

The 59th Annual Holy Convocation of the Churches of God in Christ, which ended its 10-day session in Memphis last week, witnessed the disruption of a power struggle and a subsiding of the dissension that existed within the organization. As a result the harmony, unity and fellowship for which the Saints have been known for more than half a century, was restored. Accordnig to sources, the power struggle was centered around Bishop O. T. Jones, of Philadelphia who was appointed senior bishop after the death of Bishop C. H. Mason, founder of the church. Bishop L. H. Ford, public relations director for the corporation ... said that the constitution of the Church of God in Christ does not provide for a one man leadership. "Therefore Bishop Jones was elected to his position because he was the oldest of the ordained bishops, and the church with its near 3 1/2 million members was to operate under the leadership of a twelve-member Executive Board," Bishop Ford maintained ... The executive board's claim of the total responsibilities of the Church was not accepted by Bishop Jones, his son Dr. O. T. Jones, Jr., and Bishop R. E. Ranger, Texas. This was made evident during this convocation ... During the Children's Program, the supporters of Bishop Jones staged a demonstration which stopped the service and resulted in police clearing the temple. They marched in chanting and attempting to wrest control of the platform from Bishop J. S. Bailey, who was presiding, along with other bishops and executive board members, maintained control. No physical violence resulted from the encounter. The building was evacuated in order to give the opposing sides an opportunity to come to agreement. The Executive Board then obtained a temporary injunction against Jones and Ranger, restraining them from interfering with the business and official program of the church. The church's ruling was upheld by Chancellor Charles Rond in a preliminary Chancery Court hearing on November 17. Although Chancellor Rond ruled that he had no power to intervene in the removal of Bishops Ranger and Jones, he broadened the injunction to include accounting of funds by both sides each quarter ... The General Assembly, by a vote of 907 to 3, decided that Bishops O. T. Jones and R. E. Ranger be removed from their respective offices and titles. After one year if they "repent" of their wrongs they may apply for reinstatement. All official actions taken by either Bishop Jones or Bishop Ranger during this term will be called null and void by the governing body of the Church of God in Christ. As a result Bishop DeWitt Burton was appointed to Bishop Jones' diocese of Eastern Pennsylvania, and Bishop Ranger's diocese of South East Texas will be supervised by the Executive Board of the Church until the appointment of an overseer ... Bishop A. B. McEwen was elected president of the Church of God in Christ; Bishop J. S. Bailey, vice-president; Bishop J. O. Patterson, secretary; Bishop Dewitt Burton, assistant treasurer. (Thomas, 1966, p. 1)

After the disputes and problems of the 1966 National Convocation, there was much discussion about how the Senior Bishop had been treated and how the delegates had not been allowed to hear from him. There were also some who reported that those in charge of the meeting had turned off the microphones and the lights when Jones and his supporters attempted to speak (Anonymous, personal communication(s), 1999). That these types of allegations circulated throughout the Church is evidenced by the fact that Bishop J. O. Patterson (1967) found it necessary to respond to them (without actually denying them) in a section entitled "**WAS 'BISHOP' JONES DENIED THE PRIVILEGE TO SPEAK DURING THE 1966 NATIONAL CONVOCATION**" (p. 20) which stated:

> I know it has been widely circulated that "Bishop" Jones was mistreated and denied the privilege of speaking during the 1966 National Convocation. This is far from the truth. "Bishop" Jones' effort to gain access to the pulpit to speak was denied not because the presenting officer did not want "Bishop" Jones to bring a gospel sermon, or pray for the sick or speak words of encouragement to the delegates, but because they knew that "Bishop" Jones was seeking to gain permission to speak for the purpose of arguing the charges that had been filed against him and of which he had been duly notified before the General Convocation as he had pledged to do and had published in a brochure, October 31, 1966. And from this brochure is the following quotation:
> "I shall answer my accusers, the Lord willing, before the entire church, called together especially for this purpose in the main auditorium of our national temple, at a time when everybody can hear and judge for themselves." (Patterson, 1967, p. 20)

One final court action occurred on the last day of 1966 that gave a clear indication of how the power struggle was progressing. On December 31, 1966 the *Tri-State Defender* under a headline "Texas Judge Rules In favor of COGIC Board" ("Texas Judge," 1966) told the story of how another state judge had thrown his weight behind the building case law which was unanimously supporting the position of the Executive Board. This article also adds some interesting detail with regard to who and how many supporters were gathering to the two sides in this contest to decide which organizational path COGIC would follow:

Judge Warren P. Cunningham ruled in favor of members of the Executive Board on [sic] the Church of God in Christ, following a hearing in the Harris County District Court here recently, on an application for a temporary injunction filed by Bishop R. E. Ranger of the Southeast District of Texas. The decision by Judge Cunningham is regarded by the Executive Board members as a key victory in the group's fight with a church faction representing Bishop O. T. Jones, of Philadelphia, who was ousted as senior bishop of the Church at the annual COGIC convention in Memphis last November. Bishop Ranger, who was removed from the State Bishops' Board at the same time, is a supporter of Bishop Jones in the factional fight. Bishop Jones recently held what he called a nationwide rally of support in Philadelphia and reported that "a dozen bishops and 300 ministers" of the COGIC attended. The Executive Board is supported by the more than 70 "bona fide" bishops of the Church and practically all ministers of the denomination's more than 5,000 churches throughout the United States and several foreign countries. In addition, the Board has the support of all national officers who head auxiliaries, as well as Dr. Arenia C. Mallory, president of the Saints Junior College, Lexington, Miss. Bishop Ranger had asked the court to issue a temporary injunction restraining the Executive Board from interfering with his authority and dispossessing his jurisdiction in the Church of God in Christ of Southeast Texas ... Among the bishops on hand to lend moral support to the defendants [the Executive Board], were Bishop D. Lawrence Williams, chairman of the State Bishops' Board, Norfolk, Va., Bishop J. H. Dell of Albany, Ga., secretary of the Elder's Council; Bishop E. Courtney, Trenton, N.J., a member of the State Bishops' staff, and Elder Roger Jones, of Flint, Mich., a member of the Youth Provisional Board ... Following Judge Cunningham's decision, the entire Executive Board went into special session at the Buck Street Memorial Church of God in Christ to weight [sic] the future of the Church in Southeast Texas. It was decided that the Southeast District will be administered under the jurisdiction of the Executive Board until a Bishop has been appointed. ("Texas Judge," 1966)

This concludes the summary of the circumstances surrounding the initial succession of O. T. Jones as COGIC's Senior Bishop. I have discussed his leadership style and his view of COGIC's organizational nature. I have also detailed the major accomplishments of his administration and provided the outlines, and some details of the conflict, which brought his administration to an end.

CHAPTER VII

The Circumstances and Proceedings of the 1968 Constitutional Convention

The allegations of the Executive Board and the response of the Senior Bishop (and his supporters) set the stage for a power struggle (DuBois, 1966, p. 8; Synan, 1987, p. 84; Thomas, 1966, p. 1) within the leadership of the Church of God in Christ. The great question that faced this divided leadership was, "Where the authority of the Church of God in Christ is placed by its Constitution?" (Patterson, et al., 1969, p. 77). Negotiations could not resolve the issues. In the end the matter was submitted to the Chancery Court of Shelby County, Tennessee.

On October 10, 1967, Chancellor Rond issued a Consent Decree in case 69683-2 R.D. (*Tennessee v. O. T. Jones, SR,* 1967) which stated that the parties involved "recognize and agree that the ultimate solution of ... these questions and all related ancillary questions should be determined by the General Assembly of the Church of God in Christ in a Constitutional Convention called for that purpose" (Patterson, et al., 1969, p. 86). The time set (by the decree) for this first-ever COGIC Constitutional Convention was January 30 through February 2, 1968 at the national head-quarters of the Church in Memphis, Tennessee.

This Consent Decree was accepted by four separate law firms representing the Complainants/Defendants and three separate law firms representing the Defendants/Cross Complainants. However, even though the lawyers representing his faction signed off on the agreement the actions called for by the Consent Decree were not in actuality acceptable to Bishop O. T. Jones, Sr. (D. Duke, personal communication, November 22, 1999).

The Senior Bishop chose not to participate in the Convention and refused to accept the actions or results of this convention as either traditionally or biblically correct. This immediately acted to split the Church into three uneven factions. The largest faction consisted of those who supported the General Secretary and the Executive Board who were determined upon changing the structure of the Church. The supporters of Senior Bishop Jones divided into two camps. One camp (the largest of the two) consisted of those who abstained from participation because they believed (like their leader) that the goal and the process was tainted. The smallest camp consisted of those who were determined to fight for what they believed was the traditional COGIC organizational structure as delivered directly by Bishop C. H. Mason from God (D. Duke, personal communication, November 22, 1999).

The court mandated Constitutional Convention which convened on January 30, 1968 gathered in Memphis to answer the central question, "Where the authority of the Church of God in Christ is placed by its Constitution?" (Patterson, et al., 1969, p. 84).

Bishop D. Lawrence Williams of Virginia was now the undisputed Chairman of the Board of Bishops. This came about because of a meeting that took place at the church where he was the pastor in 1966 - C. H. Memorial Church of God in Christ, Norfolk, VA. This meeting occurred when the entire Executive Board came to Bishop Williams' Church and confronted him about his outspoken support for Bishop Jones. This meeting consisted of a public meeting and a private meeting that was attended by the Executive Committee, Bishop Williams, his staff and the elders of his jurisdiction who were in attendance. According to an eye-witness at this meeting the Executive Board asked pointedly, "Do you recognize the pattern of authority in the Church?" (Anonymous, personal conversations, December 1999). When Bishop Williams saw that he was being (as the eye-witness characterized it) crucified he "asked for mercy and then recanted his support of Bishop Jones" (Anonymous, personal conversations, December 1999).

The Chancery Court of Shelby County, Tennessee had decreed that until the Constitutional Convention the Church should be under the general supervision of the Board of Bishops (*Tennessee v. Jones*, 1966). Pursuant to this Consent Decree delegates from across the United States and around the world gathered at the National Headquarters of the Church of God in Christ in Memphis, Tennessee in late January 1968. These delegates represented millions of COGIC members who expected them to settle the contro-versies, which divided the Church through the process of amending the Church's Constitution.

As the Chairman of the Board of Bishops, Bishop D. Lawrence Williams served as the temporary chair when the Convention first opened. And by the authority vested in him as the temporary chair made two of the most important appointments of the Convention.

First, he appointed Bishop Levi Willis as the chairman of the Credentials Committee. This committee was to exam-ine the records of the delegates who were issued credentials, to examine and rule upon those who were refused creden-tials and to turn a report of their findings into the Convention for approval. This Committee worked closely with the office of the General Secretary, Bishop J. O. Patterson for the reg-istration of delegates in the Credentials Committee and served as the initial entrepôt for power in the Convention

(Cornelius, 1975, p. 86; Patterson et al., 1969, p. 84; J. Williams, personal conversation, December 9, 1999). The surprising element of this appointment resides in the fact that Bishop Levi Willis had been appointed and consecrated a bishop by Bishop Jones. In a letter issued by the Executive Board dated February 20, 1967 and signed by Bishops McEwen, Bailey, and Patterson declared this appointment null and void (Patterson, 1967, p. 24).

Second, as the temporary chairman, Bishop D. L. Williams also appointed Elder John Butler, the Chairman of the Rules Committee and charged him with preparing rules and procedures to govern how the Convention should be conducted (Cornelius, 1975, p. 86; Patterson et al., 1969, p. 84; J. Williams, personal conversation, December 9, 1999).

Following these two pivotal appointments, the temporary chairman elicited nominations for a permanent Chairman. The delegates placed the names of Bishops T. D. Iglehart, W. L. Broussard, and C. E. Bennett in nomination, all of whom were supporters of the Executive Board ("Texas Judge," p. 15). Bishop Iglehart won a majority of the votes and replaced Bishop D. Lawrence Williams as the Chairman of the Constitutional Convention (Cornelius, 1975, p. 86; Patterson et al., 1969, p. 84).

Once the Convention elected a permanent Chairman, they continued to order its affairs in accordance with rational-legal forms. They nominated four men to serve as Secretary to the Convention and elected Dr. R. S. Page Secretary and Elder Herbert Williams as his assistant.

Appointments by the Chairman filled two extremely important areas. First, to conduct the many votes, which this Convention would be called upon to make tellers were appointed and instructed in the matter of impartial and accurate procedures. Second, he appointed the Constitutional Committee responsible for receiving all proposed constitutions, all amended constitutions or recommendations for constitutions which had been duly registered with the Convention Secretaries. The Constitutional Committee consisted of people from both sides of the dispute with the majority coming from the supporters of the Executive Board. The members of this Committee included; Bishop W. Wells, Chairman; Elder J. C. Griffin, Dr. O. T. Jones, Jr., Dr. M. McGregor Jones, Bishop C. W. Williams, Eld. W. Jones, Mother Anne Bailey, Dr. T. L. Pleas, Elder C. E. Cannon, and Clifton Williams. This committee had the responsibility of reviewing the materials submitted to it and then consolidating and editing them into a recommendation to the Convention. From the beginning of this committee's deliberations it was decided that both a majority and a minority report would be accepted (Cornelius, 1975, p. 86; Patterson, et al., 1969, p. 84).

The Constitutional Committee, working fast to stay within the time constraints imposed by the Consent Decree, heard presentations by several people regarding proposed amendments and new constitutions. After lengthy debate and consultations, the Constitutional Committee proposed an amendment to the Convention. The majority of the delegates voted this amendment down.

Following the rejection of the initial proposal of the Constitutional Committee the Committee debated a resolution submitted by Elder Wright of Detroit, Michigan. After a "cursory examination and scrutiny of the proposal" (Cornelius, 1975, p. 86; Patterson, et al., 1969, p. 85) this resolution became the foundation of the majority report which was then submitted to the General Assembly by the Constitutional Committee. At the same time, Dr. O. T. Jones, Jr. prepared a minority report and submitted that to the Assembly. Both reports were debated, speeches for and against each were heard and then a vote was taken. The vote was taken first on the majority report. The votes of the certified delegates were recorded as follows, 1,085 for and 286 against the proposed amendment, which reveals the comparative strengths of the Executive Board faction as compared to the attending Jones' faction (Cornelius, 1975, p. 86; Patterson, et al., 1969, p. 84-85).

The amendment as accepted follows:

Whereas, the Constitution and By-Laws of the Church of God in Christ have not been amended, modified, or supplemented; and,

Whereas, it is claimed from time to time that the Constitution has been altered by virtue of custom, usage and practice; and,

Whereas, since 1952, the Church of God in Christ has witnessed the demise of its Chief Apostle, Founder, and Senior Bishop C. H. Mason; and,

Whereas, the 1952 Constitution in Article 7 thereof provided that Senior Bishop Mason would retain his present power and authority during his lifetime and upon his death said authority would revert to the Board of Bishops; and,

Whereas, the Church of God in Christ has witnessed since 1952; as well as since the death of Bishop C. H. Mason, a great growth in its membership, its pastors, bishops, new departments and physical structure; and,

Whereas, the 1952 Constitution fails to speak to many areas in which the Church has grown spiritually, administratively, financially and numerically; and,

Whereas, the financial structure of the Church of God in Christ may have been adequate in the beginning but is wholly inadequate today because the rapid development, progress and expanding needs of the Church demand that the National Church be self-sustaining; and,

Whereas, there has developed a controversy with respect to where the authority and leadership of the Church of God in Christ is placed by its 1952 Constitution since the death of Senior Bishop Mason; and,

Whereas, on the 10th day of October, 1967, in a Consent Decree entered in Cause 69683-2 R. D. in Memphis, Shelby County, Tennessee, the parties to the controversy acknowledges "that the ultimate question is Where the authority of the Church of God in Christ is placed by its Constitution" ... and further "the parties recognize and agree that the ultimate solution of ... these questions and all related ancillary questions should be determined by the General Assembly of the Church of God in Christ in a Constitutional Convention called for that purpose;" and,

Whereas, such Constitutional Convention is now convened, pursuant to the Settlement Decree heretofore referred to, on the date stated by Chancellor Rond in his order, for the purpose of resolving the ultimate issue of authority and responsibility within the church as well as to modernize the Constitution of the Church of God in Christ in the light of its national and international growth both spiritually, administratively, and numerically;

NOW, THEREFORE, BE IT RESOLVED, that the Constitution and By-Laws of the Church of God in Christ Inc. be amended as follows:

1. That the General Assembly is the only doctrine-expressing and law-making authority of the church;
2. That a General Board of twelve (12) bishops be elected for a term of four years by the General Assembly from the Board of Bishops to conduct

the executive and administrative affairs of the church between meetings of the General Assembly; and

3. That the General Assembly elect for a term of four years from the General Board a Presiding Bishop and a First and Second Assistant Presiding Bishop. The Presiding Bishop shall be the Chief Executive officer and would be empowered to conduct the executive affairs of the Church of God in Christ between meetings of the General Assembly and the General Board, with the limitation that the action of the Presiding Bishop would be subject to the approval of a majority of the General Assembly and the General Board;

4. That neither the Presiding Bishop nor any member of the General Board can serve at the same time as an officer of the General Assembly, the General Council, or the Board of Bishops.

5. That all civil officers of the corporation known as the Church of God in Christ shall be elected by a majority vote of the members of the General Assembly, present and voting, and ecclesiastically, the heads of departments of the Church of God in Christ shall be appointed by the General Board for a term of four years, provided such appointments are approved by a majority of the General Assembly present and voting.

6. That the Office of Senior Bishop and Executive Board of Bishops be abolished.

7. That any amendment in the Constitution of the Church of God in Christ that is not consistent with the Amendment herein is hereby repealed. (Cornelius, 1975, p. 86-87; Patterson, et al. 1969, p. 85-87)

The adoption of this resolution settled the question, "Where the authority of the Church of God in Christ is placed by its Constitution?" (Patterson, et al., 1969, p. 77). This was the question, which had first raised the storm, this was the question which was at the heart of all the litigation in the Chancery Court of Tennessee as it was in other venues. And this was the question that addressed the issues set forth in the Consent Decree. Within this decree a new church polity was born, a church polity that answered this crucial question, which the vagueness of the previous Constitution and the organizational arrangements left by Bishop Mason when he died had in effect asked. It also signaled the ultimate triumph of bureaucratic organizational structure over both charismatic and traditional organizational forms. In its call for the diffusion of power through the election of a General Board, a Presiding Bishop, and a First and Second Presiding Bishop authorized to conduct the administrative functions of the Church but at the same time charged with receiving the approval of the General Assembly for their major appointments and decisions the opportunity for the authoritarian style of leadership which had been inherent in the position of Senior Bishop were circumvented.

The atmosphere of this Constitutional Convention was highly charged with political partisanship. The majority used many tactics to ensure that their points passed. At times when the minority offered reports and amendments someone turned off the microphones and lights. Other tactics, which displayed the partisan nature of this Constitutional Convention, surfaced when the majority supporters shouted minority speakers down and used parliamentary procedure to delay votes until the early hours of the morning (D. Duke, personal communication, November 22, 1999; J. Williams, personal Communication, December 9, 1999).

This was not an atmosphere conducive to a fair and well-received general election to fulfill the mandates of the newly amended COGIC Constitution. According to the Constitution, and the Consent Decree the Church was under, the general supervision of Board of Bishops and so an immediate election was not absolutely necessary. To avoid the rancor and division that an immediate election might have caused a motion that would provide the mechanism to do so had to be introduced to and accepted by the General Assembly. Elder Chandler D. Owens offered such a resolution, which the General Assembly approved and adopted (Cornelius, 1975, p. 87; Patterson, et al., 1969, p. 84-85).

This resolution required the deferment of the election of the General Board and the Presiding Bishops until a date selected by the General Assembly. This motion empowered the Board of Bishops to appoint a board of seven men to handle the administration of the Church until the time selected for the election. This motion also stipulated that the Nominating Committee, chaired by Bishop W. M. Rimson, which had previously been appointed by the Board of Bishops, would remain intact and would nominate men for election to the General Board. The General Assembly could also nominate men for election to the General Board (Cornelius, 1975, p. 87; Patterson, et al., 1969, p. 84-85; D. Duke, personal communication, November 22, 1999).

After this motion was accepted, there remained two actions which must be accomplished before the work of the Constitutional Convention could be dismissed. Consequently, immediately after Owens' resolution was accepted, the General Assembly voted to set the date for the first election of the General Board and the Presiding Bishops. This date was set for November of 1968 to coincide with the annual Holy Convocation. Following this vote Bishop D. Lawrence Williams, as the Chairman of the Board of the Bishops called a meeting of the Board and following private deliberations, the Chairman appointed seven men to serve as the Interim Board charged with conducting the administration of the Church. These seven men were, Bishop J. S. Bailey (Chairman), Bishop S. M. Crouch, Bishop L. H. Ford, Bishop O. M. Kelly, Bishop A. B. McEwen, Bishop J. O. Patterson, and Bishop Wyoming Wells (Cornelius, 1975, p. 87; Patterson et al., 1969, p. 88).

CHAPTER VIII

The Circumstances Surrounding the Election and Installation of Bishop J. O. Patterson as the First Presiding Bishop

When the 1968 Convocation convened, one person who attended was Dr. Vinson Synan, the son of Bishop Joseph A. Synan, the long-time General Superintendent of the Pentecostal Holiness Church (PHC). Dr. Synan was a university-trained historical observer, a man who was raised in the highest levels of religious leadership, and who would go on to become the General Secretary and Assistant General Superintendent of the PHC himself. He was uniquely qualified to make an informed judgement as to the circumstances of this election. His observations while attending the Convocation provide a vivid snap-shot of an organization locked in a power struggle (DuBois, 1966, p. 8; Synan, 1986, p. 48; Thomas, 1966, p. 1).

Dr. Synan speaks of a denominational meeting, "Like something never seen before in a church meeting ... it resembled a normal American political meeting ... people outside the Temple wore badges and carried signs promoting various leaders ... the atmosphere was tense" (V. Synan, personal communication, November 30, 1999).

The 61st Holy Convocation of the Church of God in Christ convened on November 5, 1968 with all the hoopla of a political convention, including placards, buttons and crowds of supporters mobbing the entrances to the auditorium (V. Synan, personal communication, November 30, 1999).

This meeting was initially presided over by the Chairman Bishop J. S. Bailey and the Interim Board. The first order of business was to develop procedures for the smooth operation of this epoch-making election. The General Assembly elected a Rules Committee to develop these procedures and guidelines. Bishops S. C. Cole, L. T. Walker, John White, and D. Lawrence Williams co-chaired the Committee, which the General Assembly charged with governing and controlling the election. The Rules Committee selected a team to pilot the convention past storms of controversy and into the calm of unity. Bishop S. C. Cole as the Election Chairman led this committee and Bishop L. T. Walker served as the Vice-Chairman. Bishop W. L. Broussard, Dr. Arenia C. Mallory, and Bishop G. B. Pickens served as the Parliamentarians. The Election Committee chose Bishop Theo Davis as the Sargent-at-Arms and, as such, he stationed Marshals throughout the auditorium to ensure that the election proceeded without any disruptions. The Chairman of the Credentials Committee, Bishop L. E. Willis ensured that all delegates were qualified and eligible to vote. Elder Chandler D. Owens chaired the Committee on Rules and Procedure for the General Assembly. Bishop F. G. Green chaired the Committee on Rules to Govern the General Board and the Presiding Bishop. Bishop Willie James and Dr. Arenia C. Mallory served as Head Tellers rounding out the election team by supervising the mechanics of the election and counting the votes (Cornelius, 1975, p. 88; Patterson, et al., 1969, p. 84-85).

At 11:00 AM on November 13, 1968, Bishop W. M. Rimson, the chairman of the nominating Committee, submitted the following names to the General Assembly as nominees for the General Board:

Bishop J. S. Baily (Michigan), Bishop C. E. Bennett (Indiana), Bishop C. H. Brewer (Connecticut), Bishop D. A. Burton (Pennsylvania), Bishop Esau Courtney (New Jersey), Bishop C. C. Cox (Nevada), Bishop S. M. Crouch (California), Bishop Theo Davis (Mississippi), Bishop J. H. Dell (Georgia), Bishop Isaac Finley (Utah), Bishop L. H. Ford (Illinois), Bishop E. E. Hamilton (California), Bishop F. L. Haynes (Texas), Bishop J. D. Husband (Georgia), Bishop Iglehart (Texas), Bishop J. E. Jeffries (Oklahoma), Bishop O. M. Kelly (New York), Bishop B. S. Lyles (Mississippi), Bishop A. B. McEwen (Tennessee), Bishop J. O. Patterson (Tennessee), Bishop E. B. Stewart (California), Bishop W. Wells (North Carolina), Bishop John White (Louisiana), and Bishop D. Lawrence Williams (Virginia). (Cornelius, 1975, p. 88; Patterson, et al., 1969, p. 89-90)

There were also the following names put into nomination from the floor:

Bishop L. T. Walker (Arkansas), Bishop L. Anderson (New York), Bishop J. A. Blake (California), Bishop A. A. Childs (New York), Bishop L. M. Driver (California), Bishop D. C. Love (Virginia), Bishop J. O. Mason (Illinois), Bishop W. A. Patterson (Michigan), Bishop F. D. Washington (New York), and Bishop L. E. Willis, Sr. (Virginia). (Patterson, et al., 1969, p. 85)

On November 14, 1968, the General Assembly of the Church of God in Christ proceeded with the election of the General Board, the first round of this two-stage election process. The Credentials Committee certified 2,151 delegates present and authorized to vote. The Committee on Rules and Procedure for the General Assembly prescribed that the delegates would vote by jurisdictions. Each jurisdiction would come forward in turn, as they walked past the Head Teller and his assistants gave the qualified voting delegate a ballot. The tellers then instructed the voters on how to complete the ballot. The tellers then collected the completed ballots and deposited them into the ballot box. Poll watchers observed this entire procedure from beginning to end. At the end of the process the Head Tellers and their assistants took the ballot box and left the auditorium to count the votes (Patterson, et al., 1969, p. 84-85).

The results of the vote, in descending order were as follows:

Bishop J. O. Patterson (828 votes), Bishop J. S. Bailey (816 votes), Bishop S. M. Crouch (810 votes), Bishop Wyoming Wells (712 votes), Bishop L. H. Ford (706 votes), Bishop O. M. Kelly (700 votes), Bishop C. E. Bennett (695 votes), Bishop J. A. Blake (600 votes), Bishop John White (579 votes), Bishop D. Lawrence Williams (561 votes), Bishop F. D. Washington (500 votes), Bishop J. D. Husband (450 votes). (Cornelius, 1975, p. 88; Patterson, et al., 1969, p. 90-91)

These 12 received the top 12 vote amounts and therefore became the first General Board of the Church of God in Christ. The other nominees received votes as follows:

Bishop T. D. Iglehart (434 votes), Bishop Leroy Anderson (400 votes), Bishop F. L. Haynes (397 votes), Bishop C. C. Cox (388 votes), Bishop E. E. Hamilton (373 votes), Bishop W. A. Patterson (349 votes), Bishop A. B. McEwen (323 votes), Bishop L. T. Walker (306 votes), Bishop C. H. Brewer (280 votes), Bishop D. A. Burton (280 votes), Bishop J. H. Dell (271 votes), Bishop Theo Davis (230 votes), Bishop Levi Willis (206 votes), Bishop L. M. Driver (177 votes), Bishop E. B. Stewart (167 votes), Bishop Essau Courtney (150 votes), Bishop B. S. Lyles (150 votes), Bishop D. C. Love (139 votes), Bishop A. A. Childs (130 votes), Bishop J. E. Jeffries (128 votes), Bishop J. O. Mason (92 votes), and Bishop Isaac Finley (38 votes). (Cornelius, 1975, p. 88; Patterson, et al., 1969, p. 90-91)

On November 15, 1968, the following names were presented by the Nominating Committee to the Chairman of the General Assembly, Bishop S. C. Cole for the posts of Presiding Bishop, First Assistant Presiding Bishop and Second Assistant Presiding Bishop:

Bishop J. S. Bailey, Bishop S. M. Crouch, Bishop O. M. Kelly, Bishop J. O. Patterson, and Bishop Wyoming Wells. (Cornelius, 1975, p. 88; Patterson, et al., 1969, p. 91)

Just as in a secular election campaign, both nominating and seconding speeches were made for each candidate (Patterson, 1969, p. 91). Following the same procedure that was used in the first round the delegates proceeded to vote by jurisdictions. It had previously been decided, that just as in the vote for the General Board, the results of this election would fill the top three executive offices in order of their respective amounts. After the votes were counted, the results, in descending order were:

> Bishop J. O. Patterson (362 votes), Bishop J. S. Bailey (264 votes), Bishop S. M. Crouch (244 votes), Bishop Wyoming Wells (51 votes), and Bishop O. M. Kelly (29 votes). (Cornelius, 1975, p. 88; Patterson, et al., 1969, p. 84-85)

Finally, after four years of turmoil, four years of conflict, the Church of God in Christ had a newly established and court-certified organizational structure. The Constitutional Convention had sketched in the outlines of a bureaucratic organization where even the highest officers were subject to the checks and balances of a non-charismatic, non-traditional organization. Thus COGIC became an organization wherein the rational-legal rule of law and the guideline of regulations would maintain a growing denomination past the problems and divisions of future leadership changes. There would no longer be any doubt about "Where the authority of the Church of God in Christ is placed by its Constitution" (Patterson et al., 1969, p. 77; *Tennessee v, Jones*, 1966).

The great constitutional controversy had been met and surmounted. With the help of civil courts and the tenacious determination of the men and women who made up the Church at that time the Church of God in Christ had avoided a major schism. There was a minor schism, which might have destroyed the Church when 14 bishops left to found the Church of God in Christ, International but COGIC did not break, though it did splinter. (For more information see Burgess, et al., 1988, p. 204.) How did the leaders steer their way past the shoals of schism? They did this by restructuring the entire organization.

In seven years, the Church of God in Christ evolved from a purely charismatic organization, which faced a contested succession, through a traditional organization with an autocratic leader, and into the steady assurance of legal-rational bureaucracy. This largest of all Pentecostal denominations now faced the world with a multiple leadership under the authority of boards, committees and the General Assembly.

With the inauguration of Bishop J. O. Patterson as the first Presiding Bishop ("Bishop Patterson," 1968) a new epoch was ushered in, and the transformation (routinization) of the initially charismatic Church of God in Christ into a bureaucratic organization was complete.

CHAPTER IX

Factors That Could Limit the Data

The Church of God in Christ had weathered the storm. What was this great storm that plunged a major American denomination into the tossing seas and windblown lanes of change? The Church of God in Christ eventually reached the crisis, which ultimately awaits all organizations founded by and built upon the outstanding gifts of one person. The charismatic founder/leader of the denomination, its Chief Apostle and Senior Bishop C. H. Mason, died and the storm began.

Within a Charismatic organization, loyalty and compliance do not flow within either a rational-legal (bureaucratic) or a traditional system. Instead a particular personality, a personality that the followers believe to be extraordinary is the recipient of their obedience. According to Martin N. Marger in his book *Elites and Masses* (1981):

> Charismatic authority is fundamentally different from either traditional or legal-rational in that it is a product of social crisis or rapidly changing social conditions. It is thus inherently unstable and eventually must give way to, or at least incorporate some elements of, either a traditional or a rational-legal system. The latter types are relatively long lasting and sustain themselves by meeting the general needs of society or by successfully creating social acceptability through control of information and ideology. (p. 17-18)

So after the death of Bishop Mason the stage was set for COGIC's transformation.

Initially the succession seemed to follow a rational-legal or bureaucratic trajectory. Appealing to the then current constitution, and apparently following what the leaders of the Church felt was the prescribed pattern, the General Assembly elected Bishop O. T. Jones as COGIC's second Senior Bishop in November 1962. This appeared to be a continuation of the first generation of leadership.

Bishop Jones had been one of the earliest lieutenants of the founder. His credentials for succession were impeccable. As a young man, he had been active as an evangelist founding many churches and laying the groundwork for several jurisdictions. Bishop Jones was also the last surviving of the original five bishops of the Church. He had founded and developed major ministries in the Church, Young People Willing Workers (Y.P.W.W.) and the International Youth Congress of the Youth Department. Jones was also a noted theologian who "put the experience of the saints into words" (Clemmons, 1996, p. 126), and "as a partner of Bishop Mason, he had helped to codify the doctrines and disciplines of the denomination" (Clemmons, 1996, p. 126).

When Bishop O. T. Jones, Sr. was elected Senior Bishop he took it very seriously. He turned the day-to-day operations of his church (Holy Temple in Philadelphia, PA) and his jurisdiction (the Commonwealth Jurisdiction, PA) over to others (most notably his son Dr. O. T. Jones, Jr.) and devoted himself entirely to visiting and traveling within the denomination. He gave every indication of a man who believed he had been elected to REPLACE Bishop C. H. Mason as the fully empowered leader of a compliant organization.

Once comfortably ensconced in the office of Senior Bishop, Bishop O. T. Jones, Sr. began to follow the example set by the founder. He began to rule the denomination in a very authoritarian manner. He made church-wide decisions and appointments of bishops and department heads without seeking anyone's concurrence or approval. In other words, he began acting just as Bishop C. H. Mason had acted with the exception that since he was not the founding, charismatic leader of a charismatic organization and was instead attempting to follow the traditions established by the founder he acted as an autocratic leader in a traditional organization.

This is where a basic dichotomy between Bishop Jones and his followers and a significant segment of the senior leadership developed. This dichotomy consisted of parallel but conflicting perceptions of the *office* of the Senior Bishop and the nature of the organization as opposed to the perception of the office of the *second* Senior Bishop and the nature of the *post-charismatic* organization. It was this dichotomy that eventually led to a crisis of leadership and the evolution of COGIC.

Bishop Jones and his followers saw the organization as one that adhered to the structure as laid down by Bishop Mason, both written and oral. This group followed the written guidelines as set forth in the Constitution of 1952 (as they interpreted them). In addition, they followed the traditions of the founder, including the tradition of a single, central leader who had full authority to personally control all levers of power.

The other significant segment of the senior leadership expressed the position that Bishop Jones was merely the ceremonial head of the church. According to the Jones' faction, this view of the honorary nature of the second Senior Bishop was not vocalized until two years after Bishop Jones election, when his authority was challenged. Conversely, the Executive Board faction contended that they had expressed this position openly and clearly at the time of Jones' election. The Executive Board faction asserted that Bishop Jones was acting without sufficient or explicit constitutional authorization. They also contended that the actual power resided in the Executive Board pursuant to the power-of-attorney, which Bishop Mason had executed on October 12, 1955.

This duality of perception led to allegations, answers, threats, counter threats, polarization, and eventually civil litigation. The litigation in turn led to a Consent Decree in the Chancery Court of Shelby County, Tennessee which mandated a Constitutional Convention directed by this decree to answer the question, "Where is the authority of the Church of God in Christ is placed by its Constitution?" (Patterson et al., 1969, p. 77; *Tennessee v. O. T. Jones, Sr.,* 1967).

This was the first Constitutional Convention ever held in the Church of God in Christ. It resulted in an amended Constitution that abolished both the office of Senior Bishop and the Executive Board. It established instead a General Board of 12 Bishops who would represent the General Assembly between Holy Convocations. It also established the offices of Presiding Bishop, First and Second Assistant Presiding Bishop who would represent the executive power of the Church. However, and this was the essential change that declared the victory of the rule of law and regulation over the personal rule of independent, autocratic leaders, this executive power was required to gain and maintain the majority approval of both the General Board and the General Assembly.

The limitation of this data exists mainly in their sources and in the highly charged emotions that still surround the events comprising COGIC's Dark Years. The primary limitation emerges from the fact that it is comprised (with the exception of court documents and newspaper articles) primarily of information (both primary and secondary, printed and oral), which has been gathered by and solicited from members of the Church of God in Christ. The lack of independent and therefore *presumably* more objective observers limits it through the survival of the factional perceptions outlined above.

The secondary limitation of the data stems from the fact that this type of information is subject to variations of memory and points of view even when it is gathered or written by contemporaneous observers. In other words, people who are intimately involved in momentous events *can* only volunteer the information they remember and *will* only volunteer what they choose. Both of these factors can lead to omissions and errors in the data.

CHAPTER X
Conclusion

Results of the Study

This work has examined a period of history in the Church of God in Christ using this case study as the basis for an exploration and examination of the theories and principles of organizational leadership both general and specific. It has looked particularly at three distinct epochs within this history.

First, this work examined the last days of the founder of the denomination, Bishop C. H. Mason (1961). This was accomplished by exploring his leadership style and the type of organization that he developed, concentrating specifically upon certain actions, which would have a direct bearing upon the coming leadership dispute.

Second, this work studied the period when Bishop O. T. Jones, Sr. served as the undisputed Senior Bishop (November 1962 to December 1964).

Third, this work chronicled the struggle for power, which ushered in four years of turmoil that engulfed and eventually ended Jones' administration. This turmoil ends only with a court mandated Constitutional Convention that fundamentally changed the structure of the denomination's organization and the election of Bishop J. O. Patterson as the first Presiding Bishop (December 1964 to November 1968). In developing this case study this work has sketched the leadership styles, organizational types and circumstantial events which precipitated, endured and resolved the period between 1961 and 1968 a period this work terms the Dark Years.

Significant Findings Summarized

Bishop C. H. Mason was a charismatic leader who used an authoritarian leadership style to personally lead and control The Church of God in Christ. Under his leadership the denomination developed and existed as a charismatic type of organization, which through the course of his long leadership (54 years) gradually developed the outer accoutrements of a bureaucratic organization without changing its basic nature. As Bishop Mason neared the end of his life, he created what he called My Special Committee or Commission to help him perform his duties. Officially instituted as the result of a power-of-attorney, which Bishop Mason executed in 1955, this Committee never became a constitutionally mandated institution within the Church.

Bishop C. H. Mason, the Chief Apostle and Senior Bishop of the Church of God in Christ, died on November 17, 1961. Upon his death and at the direction of Article 7, paragraph 2 of the then current church constitution (adopted in 1952) the power, which had previously resided in the person of Bishop Mason, reverted to the Board of Bishops.

Faced with the perceived necessity of choosing a new Senior Bishop (the existing constitution did not mandate this) the Board of Bishops decided that they needed additional time to do so. Consequently, two actions occurred. First, Bishop Mason's Committee tacitly recognized that their authority, power, and tenure died with Bishop Mason when they petitioned the Board of Bishops for a period of time to adjust business matters to the new situation, and to arrange for an orderly election of a new Senior Bishop. Second, the Board of Bishops granted the Committee's petition and extended their authority, power, and tenure for one year, from December 5, 1961 to December 5, 1962.

In early December of 1962, near the end of the 55th Holy Convocation of the Church of God in Christ, the

General Assembly voted to transfer the authority, power, and tenure of Bishop Mason's Special Committee to a committee of 12 men composed of the seven bishops who had served on the Special Committee augmented by two men chosen by the Elder's Council and three men chosen by the Board of Bishops. The General Assembly decreed that his Committee's mandate would continue until the election of a new Senior Bishop.

In the final hour of this same 1962 Holy Convocation someone (either Elder C. H. Mason, Jr. or one of the members of the committee of 12, who had previously been a member of the Special Committee, Bishop J. S. Bailey or Bishop J. O. Patterson) nominated Bishop O. T. Jones for the post of Senior Bishop. This nomination was duly seconded by several members of the committee of 12. The General Assembly then elected Bishop O. T. Jones, Sr. as the second Senior Bishop of the Church of God in Christ on December 11, 1962. The official Public Relations Department of the Church announced this election. Bishop Jones served as the undisputed Senior Bishop of the Church of God in Christ from December 11, 1962 until December 31, 1964. During this period, following the tradition of the Church, Bishop Jones acted with the same type of power Bishop Mason had exercised. He freely appointed Bishops and National Leaders through his own authority. He presided at two Holy Convocations (1963 and 1964). As the Senior Bishop of the Church, he delivered the message and received the offering on Official Day at both of these church-wide gatherings

Looking at COGIC after the passing of Bishop Mason and the initial succession of Bishop Jones in the light of leadership theory brings up the concept of continuity, office charisma and the legitimacy that adheres to administrative functionality. According to Bernard M. Bass in his widely respected work *Bass & Stogdill's Handbook of Leadership* (1990):

The charismatic leader is a hard act to follow. Institutional practices and the cultural imperatives built by the charismatic leader must replace him after he is gone ... Continuity is provided by key groups of believers and by distinctive practices and imagery in the form of visual art, ceremonies, and stories ... The office may make the leader. Apart from "office charisma" the demands of the office may greatly elevate the esteem of the officeholder ... Charisma grows from administrative routine. (p. 198)

Then an almost bewildering series of circular letters began to alert the leaders and members of the Church of God in Christ that a struggle for power had erupted in their organization.

On December 31, 1964, the General Secretary of the Church, Bishop J. O. Patterson, issued a circular letter addressed to Church of God in Christ Ministers and Laymen for Progress. This letter called for a meeting scheduled for February 3, 1965 in Memphis, Tennessee.

Senior Bishop O. T. Jones, Sr. responded in a circular letter of his own, which declared that the meeting called by the General Secretary was an unscheduled and unauthorized meeting.

The General Secretary on January 16, 1965 followed with a second circular letter stating that the Executive Board (referring here to Bishop Mason's Special Committee as later expanded at the 55th Holy Convocation) had authorized the meeting. The General Secretary's second circular letter also alleged that the office of Senior Bishop merely reflected the recognition of the bishop who happened to be senior in point of service and not an elective office. The letter further asserted that honorary recognition implied no authority in the Church and therefore the appointive authority formerly held by the Senior Bishop now resided with the Executive Board.

On January 20, 1965, Bishop J. S. Bailey, the Co-Chairman of the Executive Board, issued a circular letter that affirmed the official character of Bishop Patterson's original letter of December 31, 1964. Bishop Bailey stated that his letter constituted a response to Bishop Jones' letter of January 11, 1965 and ended by urging everyone to attend the meeting called by Bishop Patterson's original letter.

On January 28 1965, Bishop D. Lawrence Williams, the Chairman of the Board of Bishops, issued a circular letter. That asserted that the meeting called by the General Secretary (and now by the Co-Chairman of the Executive Board) had not been properly authorized. Bishop Williams also called for everyone to support Senior Bishop Jones asserting that he followed in the tradition of the founder.

On January 29, 1965, the General Secretary issued a third circular letter. This letter responded to the letter sent by Bishop D. Lawrence Williams. It stated that Bishop Williams was not the Chairman of the Board of Bishops and that his letter had been wrong when it said the proposed February meeting had not been authorized. This letter ended by saying that a majority of the bishops and pastors of the Church were planning to attend the February meeting.

After the meeting of February 1965, a document sent to Senior Bishop O. T. Jones, Sr. from the Executive Board punctuated the round of circular letters. This document asserted that the office of Senior Bishop no longer existed in the COGIC organizational structure. It further asserted that the power, which formerly resided in the person of Bishop C. H. Mason, currently resided in the Executive Board. Within the document, the Executive Board made certain concrete assertions and accusations. It charged Bishop Jones with usurping this power, declared his appointments of State Bishops and National Officers null and void, stated that the

Executive Board would appoint their own candidates to these same jurisdictions and offices. This document concluded by threatening that Bishop Jones and his appointees acted at their own risk and peril.

Senior Bishop Jones answered this document with another circular letter dated February 18, 1965. In this letter, Bishop Jones set forth a confusing argument. The confusing aspect of this response by Bishop Jones to the actions of the Executive Board lies in the fact that within it he confounds various aspects of a traditional organization type and a bureaucratic one. The response began by appealing to the written rules of bureaucracy pointing out that the General Assembly was the only body constitutionally competent to make laws or set doctrine. In addition, this document asserted that the Executive Board had acted improperly by calling a meeting without authorization. Bishop Jones followed this appeal to the rational-legal, bureaucratic form of written rules and regulations by a direct appeal to maintain the traditions as established by the founder.

At the annual 58th Holy Convocation in 1966, disruptions broke out between the supporters of Senior Bishop Jones and the supporters of the Executive Board. These disruptions halted the normal proceedings and resulted in a complaint filed by the Executive Board asking the Chancery Court of Shelby County, Tennessee to issue an injunction against Bishop Jones and his followers. This complaint contended that Bishop Jones and his chief lieutenant Bishop R. E. Ranger had been charged with impropriety and removed from office before the meeting of the 1966 Convocation. The court issued a Writ of Injunction against Bishop Jones and his supporters who then filed a series of cross complaints against the Executive Board. Then followed a series of complaints and cross complaints in the Chancery Court, which included an injunction issued against the Executive Board culminating in a Consent Decree issued October 10,

1997. The lawyers for all parties to the dispute agreed to this Consent Decree, which called for a Constitutional Convention to answer the question, "Where the authority in the Church of God in Christ is placed by the Constitution?"

This plethora of letters, meetings, documents, charges, cross charges, injunctions and decrees traces the course of the power struggle. From December 31, 1964 when the General Secretary and the Executive Committee called for a special meeting to November 15, 1968, this struggle enveloped the Church of God in Christ.

The Constitutional Convention that convened on January 30, 1968 was mandated by the Consent Decree issued by the Chancery Court of Shelby County, Tennessee dated October 10, 1965. When this convention opened it soon became obvious that the forces of the General Secretary and the Executive Committee held the levers of power. Senior Bishop O. T. Jones and his chief lieutenant Bishop Ranger did not attend the convention and neither of them were nominated in any of the elections which shaped the new *post-charismatic* leadership style and organizational type of the Church. The Jones forces at the Constitutional Convention were led by O. T. Jones, Jr. Vote after vote led inexorably to the victory of the bureaucratic party.

Following in the footsteps of the Founder, Bishop C. H. Mason, Bishop O. T. Jones, Sr. had attempted to carry on the tradition of an autocratic leader in a charismatic organization. This combined with the loss of the founding charismatic leader naturally changed COGIC into a traditional-type organization wrapped in the outward trappings of bureaucracy. This attempt to carry on the style of leadership used by Bishop Mason resonated with a predilection the first generation of COGIC leaders exhibited for a strong paramount leader who set policy and made appointments as he saw fit. However, this continuation of business as usual was challenged by a second generation of COGIC leaders who appealed to the structural forms of bureaucracy, a rational-legal system of committees, rules and regulations, which the founder had constructed to add form to what was initially and what remained until his death a charismatic organization.

Whether this second generation of leaders saw the framework of bureaucracy merely as a road to power or as the surety of collective leadership and the road to modernity and efficiency only they would know. However, objective study reveals that they used bureaucratic maneuvering and the secular legal system (which is established by and functions to uphold the rational-legal system) to work their way from the second tier of power to the first. In so doing, they changed the Church of God in Christ from a traditional organization with an autocratic leader to a bureaucratic organization with a collective leadership.

Answers to the Research Questions and Conclusions Drawn

1. What lessons can be learned from the COGIC's Dark Years?

    The first and foremost lesson that can be learned from COGIC's Dark Years is that if an organizational leader desires to see a seamless transfer of power after he passes from the scene he needs to have the mechanisms in place prior to that passing.

    The second lesson is that once bureaucratic forms have been appealed to in a power struggle those who are most adept at bureaucratic maneuver will inevitably triumph.

    And finally, when secular law courts (an inherently bureaucratic system) are appealed to in the context of a denominational (or church) power struggle those courts will avoid making a judgment and will (if at all possible) place the outcome within the hands of the legally constituted corporate church apparatus. Thus, any appeal to the secular courts automatically becomes an avenue for the triumph of whichever faction is more adroit at bureaucratic maneuver.

2. What preparations for leadership succession were taken before Bishop Mason's death?

    The preparations for leadership succession following Bishop Mason's death consisted entirely of Article 7, paragraph 2 of the 1952 COGIC Constitution, which stated:
    The General Assembly shall meet annually at the time and place designated by the Board of Bishops. The General Assembly shall elect by a two-thirds vote of those present and voting, two or more Bishops who shall hold office during good behavior, and shall have general supervision of the Church, and who shall compose the Board of Bishops, provided however, that Bishop C. H. Mason, the present Senior Bishop, shall retain his present power and authority during his life-time, but upon his death said authority shall revert to the board of Bishops (Pleas, 1991, p. 87).

3. What prevented an orderly transfer of power after Mason's death?

    Nothing, there was an orderly transfer of power from Bishop Mason to the Board of Bishops and then on to Bishop O. T. Jones, Sr. as the second

Senior Bishop. [It should be noted that in this initial orderly transfer of power from Bishop Mason to the Board of Bishops and then to Bishop Jones as the second Senior Bishop the then existing method of executive succession as outlined in Art. 7, par, 2 of the then current COGIC Constitution was not followed.

4. What type of leadership style was operating in COGIC during the Dark Years?

Initially a bureaucratic, collective leadership style held sway under a continuation of Bishop Mason's Special Committee and the Board of Bishops (November 1961 - December 1962). Following rational-legal forms this bureaucratic, collective leadership then passed to the autocratic leadership style of Bishop Jones' tenure as the uncontested second Senior Bishop in the tradition of Bishop Mason (December 1962 - December 1965). Once the General Secretary and the Executive Committee challenged Bishop Jones' authority and position, the accepted leadership style as well as the organizational type of the Church were adrift. This leadership and organizational drift continued as both sides attempted to establish complete control for themselves while at the same time attempting to restrain the other side through alliances and court injunctions (January 1966 - November 1968).

5. How has COGIC refined and institutionalized the succession process?

After the power struggle, the process was established by the Constitutional Convention of 1968, which abolished both the office of the Senior Bishop and the Executive Board settling the post-traditional succession of power on the General Board, and the Presiding Bishops. On April 13, 1971, this process was further refined when the General Assembly approved an entirely new constitution for the Church of God in Christ, Inc. This new constitution super-seded the 1952 constitution, which had been amended in 1968. This constitution states explicitly how the succession of leadership will descend in case a Presiding Bishop (according to Article III, Part II, Section A, Clause 1, Paragraph (a) the chief ecclesiastical and civil officer of the denomination) dies or becomes incapacitated. This succession mechanism is found in two places: Article III, Part I, Paragraph (A), (B) and Article III, Part II, Section A, Paragraph (c). The first applies to the civil functions and the second applies to the ecclesiastical.

1. Article III, Part I, Paragraph (A) states:

   The president shall preside at all meetings and shall make an annual report of the status and condition of the corporation to this Board of Directors. The President shall sign all certifi-cates, contracts, deeds, and other instruments of the corporation. During the absence or disability of the President, the First Vice-President shall exercise all the powers and discharge all the duties of the President.

   Article III, Part I, Paragraph (B) states:

   The Second Vice-President shall exercise all the functions of the President in the absence or disability of the President and the First Vice-President (Official Manual of the Church of God in Christ, 1973, p. 2-3).

2. Article III, Part II, Section A, Clause 1, Paragraph (c) states:

    The First and Second Assistant Presiding Bishops shall aid and assist the Presiding Bishop in discharging his Executive functions, and shall serve in their respective order if, for any reason, the Presiding Bishop does not serve or is unable to serve, until the position is filled by the General Assembly at one of its regular or special sessions (Official Manual of the Church of God in Christ, 1973, p. 5).

Answers to Six Additional Questions

1. Do the findings of this work support or reject the hypothesis?

    The hypothesis of this work is found in Chapter I. The hypothesis of this work is that insights into the theories and practices of organizational leadership will be gained through a detailed study of the leadership styles and organizational types that precipitated, endured and resolved the transitional period (1961 - 1968) in the history of the Church of God in Christ, which followed the death of its founder, Bishop C. H. Mason.

    This chapter enumerates and answers the research questions that were set forth in Chapter I to provide scope, order, and delimitation to this study. These questions are used "to explore the process that precipitated, endured and resolved COGIC's Dark Years." The answers to these questions, as well as the answers to several of the six additional questions, do provide insights into the theories and practices of organizational leadership. Therefore, the answer to this question is yes; the findings of this work do support hypothesis.

2. Does this study support or contradict previous research?

This study supports previous research. The following is a representative cross-section of the previous research about the routinization of charisma. Ronald M. Glassman and William H. Swantos, Jr. in their book *Charisma, History, and Social Structure* (1986), address the routinization of charisma by referring and commenting on the seminal work of Max Weber:

While pure or genuine charisma is personal, direct, radical, revolutionary, and extraordinary, when the charismatic *movement* is successful charisma becomes ordinary; its leadership becomes routinized, depersonalized, and deradicalized. Thus Weber writes: "Every charisma is on the road from a turbulently emotional life that knows no economic rationality to a slow death by suffocation under the weight of material interests: every hour of its existence brings it nearer its end." Charisma may be attached to an office, that is the gift of grace becomes attached to whomever occupies the office. In so becoming, it is depersonalized; but more important, in being attached to an office in an established political, religious, or military order, it is no longer radical. In such circumstances the magic or grace of Charisma can become the basis for the legitimacy of the order itself. (p. 31)

The very arguments used by Bishop Jones and his followers (that Jones was able to act as he did *because* he was the Senior Bishop) show that they

were attaching the charismatic rights and preroga-
tives of Bishop Mason to the Office of Senior Bishop
thus revealing the routinization process. It is this
process of evolution from the pure charisma of
Bishop Mason to the routinized charisma of either
the traditional (Jones) faction or the bureaucratic
(Executive Board) faction. This observation from the
case study of COGIC's Dark Years corresponds to
the findings of other organizational studies.

> In almost all the historical cases of pure
> charisma, the routinization of charisma did not
> occur within the lifetime of the charismatic
> leader. Therefore the radical nature of the reli-
> gious rejection of the existential world was
> maintained during the lifetime of the leader. As
> previously noted, when a charismatically led
> movement is successful, the nature of the
> charisma becomes modified in the process of
> routinization, and charisma is attributed to office,
> lineage, or clan. Charisma is no longer pure
> charisma in the original sense as discussed
> above; but the routinization of charisma provides
> the basis and the legitimacy for newly estab-
> lished traditional or rational-legal hierarchies
> and systems of domination, which, in the process
> of routinization, become conservative. The radi-
> cal nature of Charisma disappears with rou-
> tinization. (Glassman & Swatos, 1986, p. 34)

In attempting to analyze contemporary culture through a
psychoanalytical look at mass society in his book *Charisma*,
Irvine Schiffer (1973) looks at the problem of succession in
Charismatic organizations from the viewpoint developed by
Max Weber and states:

The basic problem with such authority was one of succession: who could take over after the demise of a leader whose charisma could be neither learned nor taught, only aroused and experienced? In substance, a charismatic leadership was characterized by a lack of continuity, by movement rather than stability, and by a disregard for public opinion. Such leadership was a calling that transcended democratic representation. (p. 5)

Again affirming the inherent instability that attends the succession of leadership within charismatic organizations, a finding that is substantiated by the findings of this work, the political sociologist Martin Marger (1987) in his book *Elites and Masses* addresses the evolution of charismatic organizations into bureaucracies when he states:

Also, if sociopolitical movements are too firmly associated with their leaders, the removal of such persons from the scene may result in the dissipation of the movement itself. To avoid this, charismatic leaders must stabilize their authority by reinforcing it with or transforming it into one of the other types. Furthermore, every governing system must eventually face the tasks of meeting everyday problems of administration. This requires a more permanent and formalized ruling structure, which in modern societies takes the form of bureaucracy. (p. 18)

This assessment of the successive stages of a charismatic organization mirrors perfectly what this work found occurred in the case of the Church of God in Christ. Bishop C. H. Mason, a transformational charismatic leader, used the trappings of bureaucracy to add the stability of a more recognized type of organizational form to COGIC. From the original meeting of the Pentecostal Assembly of the Church of God in Christ in September 1907 in Memphis, through the adoption of a church constitution and the power-of-attorney, which established the Bishop's Special Committee, these forms were universally bureaucratic. Bishop Jones, a transactional leader, attempted to carry on as an authoritarian leader in a charismatic office of a traditional organization. Throughout his administration and in the struggle for power that ended it, Bishop Jones also used the outward forms of bureaucracy to legitimize his hold on power, if not his specific style of exercising that power.

This answer could not be complete without reference to the universally acknowledged father of the definition of charismatic leadership, Max Weber. In the book *Max Weber: One Charisma and Institution Building*, which is composed of selected papers edited and introduced by S. N. Eisenstadt (1968), Weber states:

> In its pure form charismatic authority has a character specifically foreign to every-day routine structures. The social relationships directly involved are strictly personal, based on the validity and practice of charismatic personal qualities. If this is not to remain a purely transitory phenomenon, but take on the character of a permanent relationship forming a stable community of disciples or a band of followers or a party organization or any sort of political or hierocratic organization, it is necessary for the character of charismatic authority to become radically changed. Indeed, in its pure form charismatic authority may be said to exist only in the process of originating. It cannot remain stable, but becomes either traditionalized or rationalized, or a combination of both. (p. 54)

Weber here outlines the need to change the style of leadership (from transformational to transactional), as well as the type of organization (from charismatic to either traditional or bureaucratic) if stability is to be achieved.

The evolution of COGIC after Mason's death followed this trajectory, thus reaffirming the validity of, and supporting the findings of previous research. In the following passage, Weber talks about the motives for this change:

> The following are the principle motives underlying this transformation: (a) The ideal and also the material interests of the followers in the continuation and the continual reactivation of the community, (b) the still stronger ideal and also stronger material interests of the members of the administrative staff, the disciples or other followers of the charismatic leader in continuing their relationship. Not only this, but they have an interest in continuing it in such a way that both from an ideal and a material point of view, their own status is put on a stable every-day basis. (Eisenstadt, 1968, p. 54)

The actions of both factions (Jones and the Executive Board) appear to conform to these projections. Weber goes on to describe certain means of choosing a successor to the original charismatic leader, which have a direct application to the experience of the Church of God in Christ. When looking at the problem of choosing a successor Weber states:

> These interests generally become conspicuously evident with the disappearance of the personal charismatic leader and the problem of succession, which inevitably arises. The way in which this problem is met, if it is met at all and the charismatic

group continues to exist, is of crucial importance for the character of subsequent social relationships ... Designation of a successor by a charismatically qualified administrative staff and his recognition by the community. In its typical form this process should quite definitely not be interpreted as "election" or "nomination" or anything of the sort. It is not a matter of free selection, but one which is strictly bound to objective duty. It is not determined merely by majority vote, but is a question of the right person who is truly endowed with charisma. It is quite possible that the minority and not the majority should be right in such a case. Unanimity is often required. It is obligatory to acknowledge a mistake and persistence in error is a serious offence. Making a wrong choice is a genuine wrong requiring expiation. (Eisenstadt, 1968, p. 56)

This corollary to the theory of succession in a charismatic organization closely mirrors the events that occurred in the Church of God in Christ as outlined in this case dissertation. It is interesting here to reflect upon the three renditions of Bishop Jones' nomination for the office of Senior Bishop.

According to Samuel P. Nesbitt in his publication *COGIC VOICE* when one of the members of the committee nominated Bishop Jones to succeed Bishop Mason in 1962 he said that he did so because of a dream he had had the night before in which God had moved him to believe that Bishop Jones was the man to lead the Church (Nesbitt, 1965, p. 5). According to the *Tri-State Defender* (December 22, 1962), when Elder C. H. Mason, Jr. nominated Jones it was because of tradition, since he was the last of the original bishops he should serve as the next leader. Finally, according to Bishop Patterson in his booklet *Official*, when Bishop

J. S. Bailey nominated Bishop Jones he did so out of respect and honor and specifically denies the divine nature of this action. But when the Executive Committee came to believe this was a mistake it was Bishop Patterson who took the lead in expiating the wrongly chosen leader irrespective of his being duly nominated and elected.

Weber cites several other characteristics of the routinization of charisma, which (in light of the foregoing) are particularly applicable to this case study of COGIC's Dark Years:

> In the case of hereditary charisma, recognition is no longer paid to the charismatic qualities of the individual, but to the legitimacy of the position he has acquired by hereditary succession. This may lead in the direction of either traditionalization or of legalization. (Eisenstadt, 1968, p. 57)

When Jones assumed his office he proceeded to act as Bishop Mason had because this was how Senior Bishops acted. He therefore attempted to use the charismatic power he believed attached to his office thus leading the organization in a traditionalist direction. Weber also states:

> As a rule, the process of routinization is not free of conflict. In the early stages, personal claims on the charisma of the chief are not easily forgotten and the conflict between the charisma of the office or of hereditary status with personal charisma is a typical process in many historical situations. (Eisenstadt, 1968, p. 61)

The many parallels between the theoretical projections of organizational theory which deal with the routinization of charisma, previous research findings, and the results of this study show that a basic continuity between previous research and the findings of this work do exist.

As a final caveat to this discussion of the routinization of charisma within the organizational apparatus of the Church of God in Christ the author would like to reiterate the disclaimer found in Chapter I:

> **The author** of this work **in no way** attempts to address the spiritual aspects of the Church of God in Christ. This **is not** an examination of the spirituality, biblical correctness, or appropriateness of any of the actions described. **Neither does the author of this work wish in any way to cast aspersions** upon the characters, morals, or spirituality of any person mentioned within the context of either the case study or the evaluations contained here-in. **No judgements are expressed or implied** as to the motives, objectives, or reasons associated with any of the events discussed in this work.

In line with this disclaimer, the author would like to offer this final reflection upon the routinization of charisma with a denominational setting by quoting Werner Stark:

> In judging a church, the question cannot be whether it has connected with a certain apparatus of bureaucrats, but whether this bureaucratic apparatus has completely overlaid and stifled the life which it was supposed to assist and to preserve. Only where the latter contingency has become a reality can we speak of a routinization of charisma. ("The Routinization of Charisma: A Consideration of Catholicism" Paloma, 1987, p. 287)

3. Is the study conclusive or is further research necessary?

  This study is conclusive in that it confirms the previous research and theoretical models, which point to the inherent instability of charismatic organizations in the area of leadership succession. However, further research in this area is necessary on a case-by-case basis to evaluate the particular circumstances of individual occurrences.

4. What are the implications of this research to the discipline?

  This research has special implications for the discipline of organizational leadership as it pertains to two inter-related mechanisms for change, Organizational Development (OD) and Organizational Transformation (OT). These twin tools for the management of change are defined as:

> Organizational Development (OD) is a powerful set of concepts and techniques for improving organizational effectiveness and individual well-being … Organization development consists of intervention techniques, theories, principles, and values that show how to take charge of planned change effects and achieve success. (French, et al., 1994, p. 1)

> Organizational Transformation (OT) is a recent extension of organization

> development that seeks to create massive changes in an organization's structures, process, culture, and orientations to its environment.

Organization Transformation is the application of behavioral science theory and practice to effect large-scale, paradigm shifting organizational change. (French, et al., 1994, p. 1)

Organizational leadership experts working with charismatic organizations Can learn, in general, from this research, the possible dangers that await these types of organizations in the event of a disputed leadership succession. They can then use the specific examples and the analysis of them presented in this research to develop a realistic program of either OT or OD to guide the targeted organization to a position that is secure from the disruptions and confusion outlined in this study of COGIC's Dark Years.

5. Should currently accepted research practices be redefined?

No. Currently accepted research practices proved effective in this examination and analysis of COGIC's Dark Years.

6. Is there an accumulation of sub-answers and resolution into an overall answer to the research questions as presented in Chapter I?

Yes. The flow of the events from the death or removal of the charismatic founder/leader Bishop C. H. Mason to the election of Bishop J. O. Patterson, the first Presiding Bishop as related and analyzed in this work, leads to an overall answer to the grand tour question asked in Chapter I, "What lessons can be learned from COGIC's Dark Years?" The answer

is that to avoid the turmoil and confusion of a disputed succession organizations, especially organizations of a charismatic nature, need to have their succession mechanism well defined and structurally
(legally) in place before the death of the founder.

Recommendations

Based upon the results of this work, the author recom-
mends that all organizations have mechanisms for leadership succession incorporated within their existing structure
(for example a written constitution, bylaws, and practices).
That within these documents and practices there should be a
generally accepted successor in place and functioning (such
as a vice-president or first assistant). It is further recommended that through the publishing and distribution of these
guidelines, the education of its members, and regular practice all practical steps are taken to ensure that the succession
process is understood and accepted by the organization.

Glossary

The following terms are used throughout this work in reference to the Church of God in Christ and are therefore defined in terms of that particular denomination through direct reference to the current *Church of God in Christ Official Manual (1973).*

1. Holiness – Or sanctification, encompasses the idea of ethical purity and separation. Whereas salvation is considered the first work of grace, sanctification is known as the second. COGIC holds that sanctification is both an instantaneous and a continuous work of the Holy Spirit in the life of a believer. COGIC bases it belief in this doctrine on the biblical texts: Jeremiah 31:34; Ezekiel 36:25-27; John 6:45; Romans 6:4, 5:6, 11, &12; I Corinthians 6:15, 20; II Corinthians 5:17; Galatians 2:19, 5:24; Philippians 2:13; Titus 1:15; Hebrews 9:14. When this term is applied to a church such as, "This is a holiness church" it refers to a church that adheres to the holiness doctrine outlined above. COGIC considers itself to be a Holiness church (*COGIC Official Manual*, 1973, p. 46).

2. Pentecostal – This term references the belief in the third work (according to COGIC theology) of grace (baptism with the Holy Ghost). COGIC accepts salvation and sanctification as the first two. According to COGIC belief, a Pentecostal experience involves receiving the baptism with the Holy Ghost through faith in Jesus Christ with an honest and prepared heart. This baptism

is evidenced by glossolalia (or speaking with unknown tongues) and is seen as providing supernatural power to witness for Christ in a fallen world. This belief is based upon personal experience and upon the biblical texts found in Matthew 3:11; Mark 1:8; Luke 3:16; John 1:33; and Acts 1:4-8. When this term is applied to a church, such as, "This is a Pentecostal church" it is referring to a church that accepts Pentecostal beliefs. COGIC considers itself to be a Pentecostal church (*COGIC Official Manual*, 1973, p. 46).

3. General Assembly – The General Assembly is the supreme legislative and judicial authority of the Church of God in Christ. It is the only tribunal that has power to express doctrines and creeds of the Church, and its decisions shall be binding on all members of the Church of God in Christ (*COGIC Official Manual*, 1973, p. 9).

4. General Board – The General Assembly shall elect from among the Jurisdictional Bishops, 12 Bishops who shall comprise and be designated as the General Board and they shall be ex-officio Directors of the corporation. The decisions of the General Board shall be final unless the same are overruled, amended, repealed, or modified by the General Assembly (*COGIC Official Manual*, 1973, p. 4).

5. General Council – The General Council of the Church of God in Christ shall consist of all ordained elders who are in good standing with their local churches in the Ecclesiastical Jurisdictions of their respective Jurisdictional Assemblies, and the General Assembly (*COGIC Official Manual*, 1973, p. 19).

6. Presiding Bishop – From the 12 members of the General Board, the General Assembly shall elect a presiding

Bishop (*COGIC Official Manual*, 1973, p. 4). The Presiding Bishop is the Chief Executive Officer of the Church of God in Christ (*COGIC Official Manual*, 1973, p. 5).

7. Jurisdictional Bishop – (formerly referred to as Overseers or State Bishops) are appointed by the Presiding Bishop with the approval of the General Board (*COGIC Official Manual*, 1973, p. 17-18). Jurisdictional Bishops are the official representative of COGIC in respect to all church matters within their respective jurisdiction and has direct supervision over all departments and churches in his jurisdiction (*COGIC Official Manual*, 1973, p.18).

8. Board of Bishops – The Board of Bishops is comprised of all Bishops. This Board aids and assists the General Board in matters referred to it by the General Board (*COGIC Official Manual*, 1973, p. 19).

9. General Secretary – The General Secretary is elected by the General Assembly and acts as the secretary for the General Assembly and the Church (*COGIC Official Manual*, 1973, p. 6).

10. Jurisdictions – In the COGIC church structure there are several types of Jurisdictions. A Jurisdiction may be synonymous with a state (as in the case of North Dakota). Or, it may include areas within several states (the Arizona Jurisdiction for example includes all of Arizona, part of California, part of New Mexico and part of Texas). Or, there may be several Jurisdictions in one state (in Virginia for example there are three jurisdictions).

11. Holy Convocation – The Holy Convocation is COGIC's annual meeting, which lasts from November 25 to December 14 each year. This meeting was instituted by Bishop Mason and is set aside for spiritual and business purposes. The Church Constitution, nor the *Official Manual* specifically designates the dates and times of the Holy Convocation, although it is referred to in numerous places. These dates and times are however, universally known and accepted as an established tradition. (For further insights into the nature and substance of COGIC's Holy Convocation see Clemmons, 1996, p. 73-80).

12. Constitutional Convention -The first (and only) COGIC Constitutional Convention met in Memphis Tennessee between January 30 and February 2, 1968.

Several other terms that are used with reference to the Church of God in Christ which are not found in the current church manual, include the following:

13. Senior Bishop - A title only applied to COGIC's founder Bishop C. H. Mason and his immediate successor Bishop O. T. Jones. The office was removed from the Church's hierarchy by the 1968 Constitutional Convention.
14. Executive Board (or Commission) - An entity originally constituted by Bishop Mason. This board was removed from the Church's hierarchy by the 1968 Constitutional Convention.

The following terms refer to theories and practices of organizational leadership.

15. Charismatic authority - This type of legitimate authority exists when the special qualities of an individual are

respected by people who then give that gifted person the right to act on their behalf (Morgan, 1977, p. 172).

16. Bureaucratic (or rational-legal) authority - This type of legitimate authority exists when the foundation of power is the correct application of formal procedures and rules (Morgan, 1977, p. 172).

17. Traditional authority - This type of legitimate authority exists when power is vested in people who embody and symbolize the traditional values of customs and practices of the past (Morgan, 1977, p. 172).

18. For each of the preceding leadership styles there is a corresponding organizational type.

19. Rountinization of Charisma - This idea is based on the work of the social scientist Max Weber. An organization that has been founded by a charismatic leader and has operated as a charismatic organization, if it is to outlive the founder, becomes institutionalized at the point where its leader can exit and the organization's structure remains in operation. At this point, the organization no longer is dependent upon the special gifts of the founder for its policies and decisions (Marger, 1987, p. 18).

20. Transactional Leadership – This style of leadership works within situations, accepts the rules and values previously established, "promises rewards to followers in exchange for performance" (Ford, 1991, p. 21) and is basically an "exchange process" (Ford, 1991, p. 21). Thus the primary concern for transactional leaders is attaining goals by meeting the social, material and psychological needs of followers through the use of trade-offs, utilizing rewards and privileges as compensation

for desired actions and outcomes (Hackman & Johnson, 1996, p. 78).

21. Transformational Leadership – This style of leadership is characterized as "that kind of motivation which raises the consciousness of people about what they want" (Ford, 1991, p. 22). This style of leadership changes situations, changes what can be discussed, changes rules and values, and talks about goals. Transformational leaders seek to transform both themselves and their followers by envisioning new avenues for the use of human and material resources (Hackman & Johnson, 1996, p. 57) and by using inspiration to motivate followers.

References

Abate, F. (ed.) (1996). The oxford dictionary and thesaurus: American edition. New York: Oxford University Press.

Ahlstrom, S. E. (1972). A religious history of the american people. New Haven: Yale University Press.

Anderson, R. M. (1979). Vision of the disinherited. Peabody, MA: Hendrickson Publishers.

Anonymous. (1995, April 17). Mourners gather in chicago to pay respects to intl. church of god in christ leader bishop louis h. ford, 80. Jet. 8-10.

Baer, H. A. & Singer, M. (1992). African-american religion in the twentieth century. Knoxville, TN: University of Tennessee Press.

Baker, R. S. (1964). Following the colorline. New York: Harper & Ro, Publishers.

Bartleman, F. Azusa street : The roots of modern-day pentecost. Los Angeles: Self-published. Reprinted, Vinson Synan ed. (1980). South Plainfield, NJ: Bridge Publishing Inc.

Bass, B. M. (1990). Bass & stogdill's handbook of leadership:theory, reasearch and managerial applications: 3rd edition. New York: The Free Press.

Bennis W. & Nanus, B. (1997). Leaders. New York: HarperBusiness.

Bishop jones' election as head of church of god was sparked by son of late founder, bishop mason. (1962, November 22). Tri-State Defender, p. 5.

Bishop o. t. jones: philadelphia minister elected head bishop of church of god in christ. (1962, November 15). Tri-State Defender, pp. 1, 2,

Bishop patterson elected to the top cogic post. (1968, Novemder 23). Tri-State Defender, p. 1.

Bishop seeks hearing before entire church. (1966, November 12). Tri-State Defender, p. 1.

Blumhofer, E. L. (1993). Restoring the faith, Urbana, IL.: University of Illinois Press.

Briner, B. & Pritchard, R. (1997). The leadership lessons of jesus. Nashville, TN: Broadman & Holman Publishers._

Boulding, K. E. (1990). Three faces of power. Newbury Park, CA: Sage Publications.

Burgess, S. M., McGee, G. B. and Alexander, P. H. (eds.) (1988). Dictionary of pentecostal and charismatic movements. Grand Rapids, MI: Zondervan Publishing House.

Cheers, D. M. (1990, Jan. 22). Thousands mourn death of COGIC presiding bishop J. O. Patterson in Memphis. Jet, pp. 12-14.

Christian, C. M. (1995). Black saga: The african american experience. Moston, MA: Hougton Mifflin Company.

Church controversy grows - ousted bishop says his dismissal was illegal. (1966, November 16). Memphis Press-Scemitar, p. 28.

Church of god in christ approves plans to set up publishing house. (1965, December 11). Tri-State Defender, P. 13.

Church of god in christ's 56th holy convocation to start here november 25. (1963, November 30). Tri-State Defender, p. 4.

Church pays $25,000 for shrine to bishop. (1964, December 12). Tri-State Defender, p. 1.

Clemons, I. C. (1996). Bishop c.h. mason and the roots of the church of god in christ. Bakersfield, CA: Pnuema Life Publishing.

_____ (1992) Shaping the coming era of the church of god in christ in eastern new york first jurisdiction. New York: New York Theological Seminary.

Cobbins, O. B. (1966). History of church of christ (holiness) u. s. a. 1895-1965. New York: Vantage Press.

Cornelius, L. J. (1975). The pioneer: History of the church of god in christ. Memphis, TN: Church of God in Christ Publishing House.

Covey, S. R. (1990). Principle-centered leadership. New York: Simon & Schuster.

Cox, H. (1995). Fire from heaven. Reading, PA: Addison-Wesley Publishing Company.

Crayne, R. (1989) Pentecostal handbook. Privately printed in the U.S.A.

Criswell, J. W. (1998). Qualitative inquiry and research design: Choosing among five traditions. Thousand Oaks, CA: Sage Publications.

_____. (1994). Research design: Qualitative & quantitative approaches. Thousand Oaks, CA: Sage Publications.

Cunningham, R. J. (1994). "From Holiness to Healing: The Faith Cure in America 1872-1892." Church History, 43, (4), 485-500.

Damazio, F. (1994). The vanguard leader. Portland, OR. Bible Temple Publishing.

Daniels, D. D. (1992) The cultural renewal of slave religion: Charles price jones and the emergence of the holiness movement in mississippi. Unpublished doctoral dissertation, Union Theological Seminary, New York.

Damazio, F. (1994). The vanguard leader. Portland, OR: Bible Temple Publishing.

Darrett V. Church of God in Christ No. 1, of Silisbee, TX, S. E. Appellate.

Dayton, D. W. (ed.) (1985). The higher christian life. New York: Garland Publishing, Inc.

_____ (1987). Theological roots of pentecostalism. Peabody, MA: Hendrickson Publishers.

DePree, M. (1989). Leadership is an art. New York: Doubleday.

Dobson, E. G., Leas, S. B. and Shelly, M. (1992) Mastering conflict & controversy. Portland, OR: Multinomah.

Donaldson, T. and Gini, A. (1996). Case studies in business ethics. Upper Saddle River, NJ: Prentice Hall.

Drake, S. & Cayton, H. R. 1962). Black metropolis. New York: Harper and Row, Publishers.

DuBois, B. (1966, November 19). Power battling factions see no room for middle ground. Commercial Appeal, p. 8.

Eisenstadt, S. N. (1968). Max weber: On charisma and institution building. Chicago, IL: The University of Chicago Press.

Fidler, R. L. (Ed.) (April - May - June 1964). The international outlook. Los Angeles, CA: The Church of God in Christ Home and Foreign Mission Department.

Finkelstein, S. & Hambrick, D. C. (1996). Strategic leadership: Top executives and there effects on organizations. Minneapolis, MN: West Publishing Company.

Folger, J. P., Poole, M. S. and Stutman, R. K. (1997). Working through conflict. New York: Longman.

Ford, L. (1991). Transforming leadership. Downers Grove, IL: InterVarsity Press.

French, W. L., Bell, C. H. and Zwacki, R. A. (1994). Organization development and transformation. Burr Ridge, IL: Irwin.

Fulop, T. E. & Raboteau, A. J (eds.) (1997). African-american religion. New York: Routledge.

Gareth, M. (1997). Images of organization. Thousand Oaks, CA: Sage Publications.

Geisler, N. L. (1990). Christian ethics. Grand Rapids, MI: Baker Book House.

Gillies, J. (Ed.). (1981). Historical collections of accounts of revival. Fairfield, PA: The Banner of Truth Trust.

Glassman, R. M. & Swatos, W. H., Jr. (1986). <u>Charisma, history, and social structure.</u> New York: Greenwood Press.

Goff, J. R. Jr. (1988). <u>Fields white unto harvest.</u> Fayetteville, AK.: The University of Arkansas Press.

Green, C. J. (1996). <u>Churches, cities, and human community: Urban ministry in the united states, 1945-1985.</u> Grand Rapids, MI: William B. Eerdmans Publishing Co.

Griffin, L. M. "The Rhetoric of Historical Movements." <u>Quarterly Journal of Speech</u> 38 (1952): 184-188.

Grittsch, E. W. (1982). <u>Born againism.</u> Philadelphia: Fortress Press.

Hackman, Michael & Johnson, C. E. (1996). <u>Leadership: A communication perspective.</u> Prospect Heights, IL: Waveland Press, Inc.

Hall, A. Z. (1995). <u>So you want to know your church?</u> Memphis, TN: Zannju Publishing.

Hackman, M. Z. & Johnson, C. E. (1996). <u>Leadership: A communication perspective.</u> Prospect Heights, IL: Waveland Press, Inc.

Hamilton, M. P. (1975). <u>The charismatic movement.</u> Grand Rapids, MI.: William B. Eerdmans Publishing Co.

Hassey, J. (1986). <u>No time for silence.</u> Grand Rapids: Zondervan Publishing House.

Heckscher, C. & Donnellon, A. (1994). <u>The post-bureaucratic organization: new Perspectives on organizational change.</u> Thousand Oaks, CA: Sage Publications.

Historical perspectives the church of god in christ: the first hundred years. (19996, Spring Edition). <u>The Whole Truth.,</u> 12-13.

Hollenweger, W. J. (1972). <u>The pentecostals.</u> Minneapolis: Augsburg Publishing House.

Holloway, J. E. (1990). <u>Africanisms in america culture.</u> Bloomington, IN: Indiana University Press.

Hughes, R. T. (1988). The american quest for the primitive church. Urbana, IL: University of Illinois Press.

Jones, C. E. (1983). A guide to the study of the pentecostal movement. Metuchen, NJ: The Scarecrow Press, Inc.

_____. (1987). Balck holiness: A guide to the study of black participation in wesleyan perfectionist and glossolalic pentecostal movements. Metuchen, NJ: The Scarecrow Press, Inc.

Kelley, F. B. & Ross, R. R. (1970). Here I am, send me. Memphis, TN: Church of God in Christ Publishing House.

Krathwohl, D. R. (1993). Methods of educational and social science research. White Plains, NY: Longman.

Lattin, D. (1995, November - December) "In Search of the Spirit" in UTNE READER, 70-83.

Lawless, E. J. (1988). God's peculiar people. Lexington, KY: The University Press of Kentucky.

Marger, M. N. (1981). Elites and masses. Belmont, CA: Wadsworth Publishing Company.

Mark, R. (1996). Research made simple: A handbook for social researchers. Thousand Oaks, CA: Sage Publications.

Marks, R. (1966, November 18). Order restrains church faction. Commercial Appeal, p. 15.

Mason, E. W. (1991). From the beginning of bishop c. h. mason and the early pioneers of the church of god in christ. Memphis, TN: Church of God in Christ Publishing.

Mason, M. (1987). The history and life work of elder c. h. mason. Memphis: Church of God in Christ Publishing.

Maxwell, J. (1996, April 8). Building the Church (of God in Christ). Christianity Today, 40, (4) 22-27.

Maxwell, J. C. (1998). The 21 irrefutable laws of leadership. Nashville, TN: Thomas Nelson Publishers.

McEwen and jones: strong contenders in church of god in christ to be senior bishop. 1962, November 24). <u>Tri-State Defender,</u> pp. 1, 4.

Means, J. (1966, November 16). Negro bishops take feud over leadership to court. <u>Commercial Appeal,</u> p. 23.

Meister, R. J. (ed.) (1972). <u>The black ghetto: Promised land or colony?</u> Lexington, MA: D. C. Heath & Company.

Miller, D. C. (1991). <u>Handbook of research design and social measurement.</u> Newburry Park, CA: Sage Publications.

Moore, L. (1986). <u>Religious outsiders and the making of americans.</u> New York: Oxford University Press.

Morring, R. (1996). <u>Mason memorial church of god in christ: 90th church anniversary.</u> Norfolk, VA: Mason Memorial COGIC.

Murphy. L. G., Melton, J. G. and Ward, G. L. (1993). <u>Encyclopedia of african american religions.</u> New York: Garland Publishing, Inc.

Nesbitt, S. P. (1965). <u>The church of god in christ voice.</u> Jacksonville, FL: Church of God in Christ Western Florida, Inc.

New leader must be selected for world-wide [sic] body. (1961, November 25). <u>Memphis World,</u> pp. 1, 4.

Nichol, J. T. (1966). <u>Pentecostalism.</u> New York: Harper & Row Publishers.

Noble, M. (ed.) (1985). <u>Like as of fire.</u> Washington, D.C.: Middle Atlantic Regional Press.

"Opinion" (April, 1968). <u>The Whole Truth.</u> P. 6.

Owens, R. R. (1998) <u>Speak to the rock.</u> Lanham, MD: The University Press of America.

Paloma, M. (1987). Charisma, routinization, and institution-alization: an exercise in weberian sociology [Monograph]. <u>Probing Pentecostalism: Society for Pentecostal Studies 17th Annual Meeting,</u> 268-300.

Patterson, J. O., Ross, G. R. & Atkins, J. M. (eds.) (1969). History and the formative years of the church of god in christ. Memphis, TN: C.O.G.I.C. Publishing House.

_____. (1967). Official. Memphis, TN: Church of God in Christ Publishing House.

Patterson, W. A. (1970). From the pen of bishop w. a. patterson. Memphis, TN: Deakins Typesetting Service.

Patton, M. Q. (1987). How to use qualitative methods in evaluation. Newbury Park, CA: sage Publications.

Payne, W. J. (ed.) (1995). Directory of african american religious bodies. Washington, D.C.: Howard University Press.

Pegus, D. S. (1984). Managing conflict god's way. Los Angeles, CA: Whitaker House.

Peters, T. 1987). Thriving on chaos. New York: Perennial Library.

Pleas, C. H. (1991). Fifty years achievement from 1906 – 1956: A period of history of the church of god in christ. Memphis, TN: COGIC Publishing.

Power fight expected at cogic convocation: church meet here may be a small 'vietnam.' (1966, November 5). Tri-State Defender, pp. 1, 4.

Pugh, D.S. & Hickson, D. J. (1993). Great writers on organizations: The omnibus edition. Aldershot, G.B.: Dartmouth.

Range, C. F. (1992). Church of god in christ: official manual. Memphis, TN: Church of God in Christ Publishing.

Reid, M. L. (1961, November 25). Bishop mason burial during convocation. Tri-State Defender, p. 1.

Robeck, C. M. (1995). The colorline was washed away in the blood. Costa Mesa, CA: Christian Education Press.

Ruling is due today in church dispute. (1966, November 17). Commercial Appeal, p. 19.

Sanders, C. J. (1996). Saints in exile. New York: Oxford University Press.

Sanders, J. O. (1994). Spiritual leadership. Chicago, IL: Moody Press.

Schiffer, I. (1973). Charisma: a psychoanalytic look at mass society. New York: The Free Press.

Senior bishop's post is honorary, says judge. (1966, April 9). Tri-State Defender, p. 4.

Sernett, M. C. (ed.) (1985). Afro-american religious history: a documentary witness.

Simpson, G. E. (1978) Black religions in the new world. New York: Columbia University Press.

Slife, B. D. & Williams, R. N. (1995). What's behind the research: discovering hidden assumptions in the behavioral sciences. Thousand Oaks, CA: Sage Publications.

Spradley, J. P. (1980). Participant observer. New York: Holt, Rinehart and Winston.

_____. (1979). The ethnographic interview. New York: Holt, Rinehart and Winston.

Synan, V. (1997). The holiness-pentecostal tradition: Charismatic movements in the twentieth century. Grand Rapids, MI: William B. Eerdmans Publishers.

_____. Ed. (1997). Aspects of pentecostal-charismatic origins. Plainfield, NJ: Logos.

_____. (1986, June). The quiet rise of black pentecostals. Charisma, 45-48.

Sypher, B. D. (1997). Case studies in organizational communication. New York: The Guilford Press.

10,000 delegates note progress of city; welcomed at hotels. (1964, December 19). Tri-State Defender, p. 1.

Tennessee v. Jones (Shelby County Chancery Court, 1966).

Texas judge rules in favor of cogic board. (1966, December, 31). Tri-State Defender, p. 15.

Thomas, D. A. (1966, November 26). Power fight simmers as 59th convocation ends. Tri-State Defender, pp. 1, 2.

Townsend-Gilkes, C. (1982). Cultural constituencies in conflict: religion, community reorganization, and the rise of the saints. Unpublished manuscript.

25,000 view bishop mason's body; 7,000 attend funeral. (1961, December 2). Memphis World, p. 1.

Wacker, G. (1984 July / October). "The Functions of Faith in Primitive Pentecostalism" in Harvard Theological Review, 77, (3-4), 353.

Washington, J. R. (1984). Black religion:the negro and christianity in the united states. Lanham, MD: University Press of America.

Washington J. R. (1973). Black sects and cults. Garden City, NY: Doubleday.

Weber, M. (1976). The protestant ethic and the spirit of capitalism. London, GB: George Allen & Unwin LTD.

_____. (1964). The theory of social and economic organization. New York: The Free Press.

Weeks, D. P. (1989). A thesis on the history of the cogic/bishop charles harrison mason, and those who helped make the history. Unpublished manuscript.

Williams, J. (1991). The church that jesus builds: A historical perspective. 85th Church Anniversary Mason Memorial Church of God in Christ. 23.

White, C. C. & Holland, A. M. (1969). No quittin' sense. Austin, TX: University of Texas Press.

Who will take over bishop mason's role as church's leader? (1961, December 9). Memphis World, pp. 1, 4.

Woodson, C. G. (1992). The history of the negro church. Washington, D.C.: The Associated Publishers, Inc.

Woolfolk, N. (1997). Centennial celebration: 1897-1997. Chicago:IL: The C. H. Mason Historical Society.

Yin, R. K. (1994). Case study research: Design and methods. Thousand Oaks, CA: Sage Publications.

Young, C. (1991). Special Editorial. <u>85th Church anniversary of mason memorial church of god in christ,</u> 14.Zikmund, W. G. (1991). <u>Business research methods.</u> Chicago: The Dryden Press.

Printed in the United States
200352BV00002B/35/A

9 781591 602897